T0194066

LOVE WILL PREVAIL
Only with God's Grace

LOVE WILL PREVAIL

Only with God's Grace

Dieuna and Luther Chrispin

WESTBOW
PRESS®
A DIVISION OF THOMAS NELSON
& ZONDERVAN

This book is a work of non-fiction. Unless otherwise noted, the author and the publisher make no explicit guarantees as to the accuracy of the information contained in this book and in some cases, names of people and places have been altered to protect their privacy.

Scriptures taken from the Holy Bible, New International Version®, NIV®. Copyright © 1973, 1978, 1984, 2011 by Biblica, Inc.™ Used by permission of Zondervan. All rights reserved worldwide. www.zondervan.com The "NIV" and "New International Version" are trademarks registered in the United States Patent and Trademark Office by Biblica, Inc.™

WestBow Press books may be ordered through booksellers or by contacting:

WestBow Press
A Division of Thomas Nelson & Zondervan
1663 Liberty Drive
Bloomington, IN 47403
www.westbowpress.com
1 (866) 928-1240

Because of the dynamic nature of the Internet, any web addresses or links contained in this book may have changed since publication and may no longer be valid. The views expressed in this work are solely those of the author and do not necessarily reflect the views of the publisher, and the publisher hereby disclaims any responsibility for them.

Any people depicted in stock imagery provided by Getty Images are models, and such images are being used for illustrative purposes only. Certain stock imagery © Getty Images.

ISBN: 978-1-9736-1999-4 (sc)
ISBN: 978-1-9736-2000-6 (hc)
ISBN: 978-1-9736-1998-7 (e)

Library of Congress Control Number: 2018902208

Print information available on the last page.

WestBow Press rev. date: 07/16/2020

Dedication

Luther II, Jubilee, Sallie, and Leena. We love you.

To the young woman and men who will marry our son and daughters.

To my mother, Dieula Alce Philippe, who taught me the value and power of family, and through whose example all her children have come to know the virtue of family for themselves.

And

To all couples, to those who are single and would want to be in a serious relationship in life. This book can be applied to everyone out there, so you will understand that you are not alone.

Whichever category you find yourself in:

Young, Single

Engaged, Newlyweds

<u>TO OUR LORD JESUS CHRIST, IN WHOSE NAME ALL HAVE BEEN MADE POSSIBLE.</u>

Foreword

Every so often, one meets ordinary people who go beyond the call of duty to volunteer in doing extraordinary things to help others and doing so despite sacrifices in time and resources. Such voluntary actions go a long way in driving communities to a higher purpose and greater destiny.

The Family Life Ministry, of the First Seventh-Day Adventist Church of West Palm Beach, has made it part of their mission to reach out to help others. Active in this effort is the husband-wife team of Luther and Dieuna Chrispin. Both quiet and mild-mannered in demeanor, it is very evident that they approach their tasks with a spirit of humbleness that bespeaks their Christian character as exemplified by the Apostle Paul: "Let us not become weary in doing good, for at the proper time we will reap a harvest if we do not give up." (Galatians 6:9)

Equally important is the way this couple live their lives as Christians. To the observer looking on, one sees the closeness of their family-exuding love, and care. Inherent is the belief that the family that prays together stays together. It is how one lives his/her life that has that powerful impact on others. This couple provides a visibly good example of the way forward.

-Dr Basil K. and Jean M. Bryan

Acknowledgments

Many years ago, my husband and I took a leap of faith into marriage. We didn't fully know where it would lead us due to so many challenges that were presented before us. Having the faith and the courage to move forward base on our love for each other and the understanding of God's mercy through Jesus our Savior, and although things wasn't easy in the beginning, God's love overcame, and He has been leading our family into fulfilling His will.

We never dreamed that God would use us to influence so many other people. We are humble and grateful that God would choose to use us to communicate anything on His behalf, particularly in leading the Family Life Ministry in our local church. We acknowledge Jesus, the beginning and the end. He is the good Shepherd who keeps His covenant of love to untold generations of those who love Him and keep His commandments.

JESUS IS THE WAY.

Introduction

Love, Relationship, Marriage- Most of us long for a good relationship, but we don't understand the deep meaning of it simply because all of us are affected by relationships one way or another.

Marriage is the most important decision a person will make, second to the decision to follow Christ.

Marriage is more important than anything we can see or feel, yet we give more meaning to everything else than we do our marriage. We put more thoughts into achieving our personal dreams and goals but neglect the very first institution God created for us. We spend more time and money into buying our dream house, yet you can't live in it if your marriage is in shambles. You are, therefore, not at peace in your own dream home.

I believe our generation has it backwards. I was fortunate to grow up in a family which places great importance on family values no matter what household income-type one belongs to. Family comes first - above work, material things, or other responsibilities. I have witnessed in other families the disadvantages of putting everything else above relationship- work, career, dreams; material things became more important than marriage or relationships. Thus, they end up having a dysfunctional family, where cars and houses are lasting longer than marriages simply because we jump in and out of marriages without proper appreciation of the institution of marriage. We, oftentimes don't have the right information about relationship or marriages. Nevertheless, we do have the tools because God gave us the tools. However, having the tools and not knowing how to use them is no different from not having them at all. We must ask God for wisdom, guidance and understanding for our marriages.

And here's a shocker.

Religious people give you a reason not to forgive a spouse who has sinned against you but to just move on with life as if nothing happened.

But heavenly **Kingdom living** tells you to forgive your spouse because where sin increased, grace increases. For if you forgive other people when they sin against you, your Heavenly Father will also forgive you.

It's amazing how many passages in the Bible there are about forgiveness, which I believe is the key to God's Kingdom.

Some couples are embarrassed to admit the way they feel about the person they share their lives with. Too often in marriage when there is offense, distrust, and conflict we identify our mates as the enemy and forget that the real enemies are the powers of darkness and our own flesh. These are the unseen enemies that we battle with. That's why Jesus wants us to forgive, so we can help each other fight the unseen war. Instead, we crucify each other daily. We leave each other in the middle of the fight to continue fighting alone while we try to save ourselves as if God only wants us to make it to Heaven by ourselves.

The power of darkness intends for our marriages to be destroyed, but when we commit to God we will wrestle with the forces of darkness, for we are not fighting against flesh and blood but against the evil ruler and authority of the unseen world.

Forgiveness can be hard and painful when it involves someone you are so madly in love with. It is the reason we become hypocritical with our own selves to the point of telling our spouses, "It's okay, don't worry about it. I'm fine," and move on with our tasks even when pain, bitterness, anger, and resentment plague our hearts. We continue as if forgiveness is a lip service.

Forgiveness is not being numb to the pain, it's not forgetting the offense, and it's not choosing to inflict the price for the offense.

When we forgive, we need to honor God with our hearts and not with our mouths.

This book aims to educate everyone what the institution of marriage truly is, hoping that by sharing our experiences we will inspire other people to give importance to their relationships, their marriages, and be truly happy and peaceful.

I. Self Discovery

Hi, my name is Dieuna, I am young, I possess many talents and I finally reached the point where I started to discover myself and decided to get to know myself a little more.

Who am I? Why am I here? What do I feel inside and why do I feel so?

I discovered lots of treasures and qualities that I didn't know I possessed. There were lots of different feelings I had buried and moved on as if they were not a part of me, as if I were someone else. These buried qualities are what brought me here and what made me who I am today.

I have been sad, angry, confused, nervous, afraid, lonely, frustrated, hurt, being taken advantage of, making the wrong choices. I have left those memories behind pretending as if I was somebody else and that I have never been there. I refused to relate to anyone going through something similar. These are all the emotional adventures that made me unfold my gift, that lead me back to where I came from, the events that brought me to where I am now. These emotional adventures brought me from one period of my life to another.

Through all the trials and opportunities, I developed a view of the world. It fostered my personality, honed my skills and my gift, and brought me my accomplishments. I overcame my own hurdles and found my victory in Christ.

I came to realize that I am here for a reason. I was born with a gift to offer the world, but instead I got lost searching for a gift *in the world*. I think many of us suffered from miseducation. We have been educated right out of our own self; we have been trained not to trust ourselves. We've been conditioned not to believe in ourselves, we've been brain-washed not to know ourselves.

The society, the environment, the culture, and our circumstances have forced us to believe that we're incapable of doing something bigger and greater than who we were born as. They tell us to stay in our place, to not cross the line and we've come to accept that. We were imprisoned until one day we discover our inner selves, our greater selves. That introduction to our own selves, to me, came from God, my creator, who created me in His own image, in His own likeness, with a gift to do His will, to be a leader and to lead by example for His glory.

I get tired of waiting and watching things to happen when God gave me the capacity to make things happen, but only through prayer and a relationship with my Creator, through my Lord Jesus Christ however our Culture trained us to look, wait and follow.

My gift and my dreams are bigger and greater than what other people tell me. I got a seed of faith that circumstances, and opposition can't stop because it's planted inside of me

My future does not depend on my circumstances or my environment. It depends on what's inside of me. The very thing that tries to stop me is what God used to make me strong and grows me out of a concrete that becomes my fertilizer. People can't cover my gift no matter what they say; if there is a seed a tree grows.

I had the privileged to watch myself outside of myself. "How is that possible?" one may ask and "how torturous that must be?"

Here's how it all started.

When I was about twelve years old, I had this great passion of becoming a writer and a dream of becoming a wife, having a family of my own without all the family dysfunctions I witnessed in my environment. That family dream was stripped off from me by circumstances at the age of fourteen and the passion of becoming a writer was second-guessed by my environment. The society in which I grew up confirmed it when I couldn't get the education I needed. I couldn't speak nor write the language. Suddenly, I found myself as a foreigner in a new country with dreams and passions that seems unreachable.

But deep inside me I discovered the gift I must offer the world, my inner power which I was created with, my dreams and passion waiting to burst out, but found that my flesh suppressed them because of self-doubt. So, I find myself fighting within myself, my Spirit, and my flesh. All the while, I blamed the society and the environment I was in because they wouldn't give me what I thought belonged to me. But the reality is, the society and the environment didn't have anything to offer me, instead I was created to bring something to the society, to my generation. My environment was waiting on me to give back something, the gift that I was born with.

If we don't know who we are, the society doesn't make it easy for us to find out. They don't want us to know; in fact, they will program you to keep you busy so you don't have the time to find yourself, until we finally get the courage to bring forth what's inside of us based on a self-awareness of our source and our purpose for being here.

We are all born with a leader inside of us. We all have the nature of a leadership spirit deep inside, although most of us become followers to others who had discovered themselves, but because of our culture we learned to bury our gifts quickly. We were trained to suppress them, to just cooperate, to be submissive by what's around us. These come by intimidation, by threats, and by instilling fear in us if we resist.

The culture has put a bridle in our lives, which tells us not to go in a certain direction and with a threat they will give us pain, shame us because of the trials and tribulations we faced in our journey. By the grace of God, we cast off that bridle, we no longer live for ourselves but to glorify God the Almighty, who redeemed us.

We no longer look at who or what's around us. We look to God because only in Him we find our strength.

And we capture ourselves in God the creator, our source.

We give birth to the strength, the courage, and the gift He planted inside of us.

Welcome to our inner world, the story of our lives. It's a story worth telling.

When we look at ourselves in the mirror, we see you because we can relate to you.

Like Job, we must lose everything in order to be rewarded with a double portion of everything that we had lost.

All right fastens your seatbelt, you are in for a great journey.

God should be the center of all marriages

God

Husband   Wife

A CORD OF THREE STRANDS

II. At the Beginning...

Adam and Eve's story is one of my models of having a successful marriage. Although their story is over 3,000 years old, I believe that there are tons of lessons we, as modern couples, can still learn from their relationship. Although Adam and Eve had been pictured with the introduction of sin, death, separation, and deception into human existence, we should also look at them as an example of a healthy couple built on understanding and resilience. There are some great lessons in their story for both couples and singles.

There is a sense of equality there, a give and take, and forgiveness. As much as people would like to take Eve out of the picture because of how we view Eve as the troublemaker, there is no where in history that I have ever heard of "Eve's story" or "Adam's story," as separate individuals. It's always about and will always be "Adam and Eve" one story together. They faced great challenges, separation for periods of time, but they always reconciled. They learned to heal ruptures together. They made a choice to be with each other over and over again. Love is a constant act of revising and retelling the story and one cannot do it all alone, it must be with someone. A great relationship could end because of death, separation, or divorce. Adam and Eve created the first great love story for you and me.

Marriage is like a stair way.

The first step is always the easiest, but you will face challenges as you go up. It is always up to the individuals to climb them all the way up as a couple, through all the challenges, together. One step at a time.

The great news is you are not alone.

There are some who like to take the short cuts in life. In case you take the elevator for a faster ride in life - whether it be in school, career, relationship, marriage, or anything for that matter, if the elevator keeps on moving up you are okay.

But if the elevator is stuck in just one floor, that's when you're in trouble.

Marriage is not an elevator. It's not a fast ride. Even though we have ups and downs, marriage is a growing process. Sometimes we might have to slow down, but we must keep on moving. In marriage we will have a down time but as long as we are moving forward together, we're okay. Lingering around one situation or phase is the problem. We must create excitements in our lives to keep us moving forward.

There are other couples who might be just like you, who are trying to make their lives or their marriages work. Nobody has got it all figured out.

We all know that marriage is not an easy task. I personally know that whatever doesn't break me will eventually make me better. I also believe that the hardship in my life is not to break me but rather to prepare me for the task ahead of me. That's my philosophy because I don't give up easily.

My word to you is to take heart, be courageous and be strong, for it is God who created marriages for our own good and that will never change. Marriage, or relationship is a great thing but often misunderstood. We don't try hard enough to discover the good that is yet to come.

Good things don't just happen, you need to go for it and make it happen. We need to thrive for the best and be patient because good things don't happen overnight either.

As a married woman, I do clearly remember the times when I was young and single. Please don't judge me based only on my marital stature, meaning just don't look at me now and draw your own conclusion as if I don't know what it's like to be in a teenager's shoes or a single lady's shoe. Been there, done that and I had my share of the struggles as well. I made mistakes that I'm not proud of. My hope in God gave me strength to move forward and I learned to make better decisions along the way.

Marriage Is Not A Sprint, It's A Marathon

III. Part of My Memoir. A Very Unclear Task

When I was twelve years old, I noticed the life my father had with my mother and I said to myself that when I grow up, I want to be like my mother. I loved my father, we had a great relationship, but I didn't want a husband like him. Why? He was married to my mother, but he also had many - not just one - but many mistresses and children all over the place. With our different needs and wants, our differences in personalities, my father was forced to pick sides every once in a while.

I don't know if that was a blessing or a curse, but I didn't want that blessing; neither did I want that curse.

I must admit that although I didn't want a husband like my father, I longed for a marriage like my parents. Their marriage was unbreakable despite all the hardships. I watched my mother day after day living her life with a purpose, a purpose to love my father and to have her children come home to their father on a daily basis. That's the value, the memory and the legacy she built into her seven children. I admire my mother for her courage. That's who I learned my family values from.

I witnessed my father's lifestyle changed completely because of the persistence of my mother's love for him. She stood by him 'til the end of his life. She's the definition of "till death do us part." What fascinated me is the fact that she's very knowledgeable about life, yet she didn't have the opportunity to get a formal education. I salute her for allowing God to shine on her and be her educator through the Holy Spirit.

I watched on many occasions where my mother should've given up on my father, but she didn't, because she was no longer living for herself alone, but for the future generations - her children.

In my early teens, I had this big dream of how I wanted my life to be when I grew up. My siblings and I were fortunate enough to grow up in the country. One evening as some of my siblings and I were outside, we laid down on the grass looking up at the beautiful stars on the sky. As we were looking up at the sky and talking about life, we recognized what was happening in our circle and how some of our older siblings and friends were getting into trouble because of their choices. I wanted to be different.

I told them that I wanted to wait before I started dating anyone because I want to meet that one boy that I'm going to spend my entire life with. I was going to wait until I was old enough to get married before I started dating. Therefore, I won't have to date here and there before finding the right one. Take note, I said the "**right one**", not **Mister Right**.

I made my wish clearly to God and before some of my siblings saying, "When I grow up, I want to have a husband who loves me for me and me alone, to have two children, a girl and a boy, that's all."

That wasn't too much to wish for. Instead, it was too little to wish for. I mean, how could I not wish to have lots of money? Silly me, leaving this earthly treasure out of my wish. Well, I had my reasons then.

My father was a fortunate man. Growing up, my father was the richest man I knew in town. He had lots of money and with lots of land. He was a farmer and so much more, where almost 90% of the people in the village were working for him, or somehow needed his help to cultivate for themselves and their families.

To my understanding, it was because of his money that he was having all those women falling into his arm as their way of survival.

They didn't care about having a husband of their own. It was just a way to survive, having children by my father, not to mention that some of the women already had a man in their lives. My father was the man with the money, and my poor mother, what can the woman say? Nothing. Whether she likes it or not, she couldn't say anything.

I love my mother. She's a very intelligent woman. She taught me how to be strong and to always look at the bigger picture. She said to me once that in every situation there is always a greater situation. We must choose. Therefore, she made a choice to stay for the sake of her children, and besides that my father loved her.

I grew up with the thought that men think they are the most powerful force in the world and if they have the money to prove it, they will think they own the world. So yes, that's the reason why I didn't want a man with lots of money. Just to have enough to survive was good enough for me. I didn't want to be owned by any man, I wanted to be loved. And I strongly believe that whether I witnessed love through my parents' relationship or anywhere else didn't matter to me because I believe that I was created with that longing to be loved. So, I refused to settle for what I witnessed in my circle and I asked God for more than what I witnessed around me.

> ## *Don't Let No One Experience Become The Source Of Your Information*

My parents were not Christian, so I didn't grow up in a Christian home, but my school had church services every Sunday and my siblings and I had to attend Sunday school. If not, when we got to school on Monday morning, we would be in trouble from the Principal who was also the pastor of the Church.

Two years later, at the age of fourteen I got ill. There was something – a cyst - growing inside my stomach which caused me to have surgery. That cyst grew inside me for a good amount of time;

every now and then it would give me a very painful stomach-ache. I would feel my stomach rise and after about 5-10 minutes, my stomach would go down and the pain went away.

I thought it was time for me to have that "monthly thing" If you know what I mean. But it was not so, the reaction was not normal, and the pain kept getting stronger and stronger. I told my mother about it later-on because she was not present when it first happened. When she looked at me I looked fine and to her understanding, kids exaggerate things. After a couple of weeks later, while I was cooking, the pain came back, and I was in so much pain that I was unable to stand straight. I went to a room close by, laid down and had one of the girls who was around at that moment stand on my stomach pressing on it, so it could go down. After a while it would go down until the next time it decided to rise-up again. That went on for a couple months until one day it was out of control. My mother got to witness me going through the pain. She was shocked and speechless. She quickly sent for my father. Before I knew it, I was in a clinic. The doctor said I needed greater care, they needed to take me to a hospital. When my parents and I got to the hospital, they were told that I needed to have surgery right away, without question. The doctor explained that there was this big, black thing growing inside my stomach which covered my ovary. Without the surgery I could lose my life and with the surgery, I wouldn't be able to conceive because they had to remove my ovaries as well.

Oh, no! I cried my heart out. In our culture, if any woman can't bear children nobody would want to marry them. People would look at me as if I'm not a woman. I had seen cases like that all the time.

If a woman looks pretty, a man would get her as a concubine but not as a wife. I had this big desire in my heart and soul of becoming a wife and a mother, having my own children one day. I cried my heart out. I didn't want to be a concubine.

> *Complaining change nothing but reaffirming your failures*

Neither the doctor nor my parents knew about my big dream and being only fourteen years old, I couldn't make my own decision. My parents had no idea of this big dream I have inside of me, and even if they knew, I don't think they would give me the choice of choosing between death or having a family. What parent would really do that? So, I came to understand. If they knew and ask me, I would probably have rejected the surgery because I had my focus in having a family of my own, and that dream was at risk.

I was only fourteen years old at that time. My parents didn't want me to die but they didn't know my dreams of having a family of my own was about to die.

I went through the surgery, went through the healing process with anger I couldn't even express or to even allow it to show. I was depressed and angry with myself and with God because he knew what my heart desired. He allowed me to go through this struggle where my heart would be crying out day and night. I couldn't erase these feelings and longing of having my own husband and children. I was dealing with this silent pain alone and felt like nobody understood. There was no counsel, nobody talked to me to bring my confidence back up. I had big dreams but lost hope of them all and there was no word of encouragement. Instead, everybody believed what the doctor said to be true. There's no hope, so what's the point of trying to be a good girl? I gave up, and besides, to my understanding, I wouldn't be good for any man anyway.

I lost hope, I lost myself, my values, my confident, my deepest feelings and thoughts, my wishes, dreams, the words of my inner world. I struggled a whole lot because I didn't know how to own my emotions. Instead, I denied its presence and pretended as if everything was great. But deep down inside I was dying.

Instead of accepting the situation and say "Yes, this is how I feel about it," and admit that I was irritated, hurt, angry, and sad, I just took actions when I should have taken time to think through the situation.

I was filled with the fear of failure. I was so afraid of losing the game of life. So, I took the easy way out, thinking that I could make things happen in my own way and get what I wanted out of life without the consequences. Without thinking that my life was already pre-destined before me, and yes, I could choose to do what I wanted and how I wanted to do it, but anything outside the Creator's plans, will result in DESTRUCTION.

And if I choose to do things according to His plan and will for my life, I will only reap the good benefit out of life. It's up to the individual to choose.

I didn't know any better.

Negative thoughts and feelings about myself and my situation would take me over completely and as a result. I made some poor choices. When I turned sixteen, I bought in to a boy who lied and told me that he loved me and I shared a part of me with him, which did not belong to him at all. I later realized that I settled for less. I didn't know my value. I didn't know my worth more than what he told me because I later found out he also loved another girl.

I realize that love is not just a word of mouth.

So, is it true that I won't be good enough? I thought he said he loved me, I shared my dreams with him, but he didn't share his dream with me. How could I be so blind and did not see through that? I thought I lost my confidence, my value after the surgery, but now it's evident that I lost everything, because I'm walking around feeling completely damaged and wasted.

> *Night makes you hope for day, and struggle makes you hope for deliverance*

IV. Unworthiness, Inferiority

Probably the most common self-doubt is a deep sense of unworthiness, continuous feelings of anxiety, inadequacy, and inferiority. There was a voice constantly speaking in my head saying, "You are not good enough and will never be good enough, everything you do is wrong. No one will love you!

Yet, I felt as if my inner self, my spirit was stuck in the wrong body. My inner self didn't match what I was going through emotionally and I was confused.

Although I was going through all these different emotions, I still had the very same feeling about my dreams, to have my own family one day.

Then I realized that I didn't lose my inner self and my feelings, they were always there but I was too busy focusing on my problem instead of listening to God. I later learned that the Bible encourages us not to be hasty in dealing with our emotions.

Life is too short to be waste in time you have already lived

The wisest man who ever lived said in Proverbs 29:11 **"Fools give full vent to their rage, but the wise bring calm in the end."**

I was that fool, I gave full vent to my anger. That caused me to get involved with the wrong people because I was angry and I was searching for answers without a clear mind and understanding.

And when I found out that my father and my brother had applied for a U.S. visa for me and my siblings, I felt a sense of deliverance from my situation. In about a year or two, the visas were granted. Six of us came to America together. Some of us stayed with my brother and some with my sister, who were here before us.

A couple of months later we got bad news, my father was ill. He came to the United States for treatment, but unfortunately the cancer had already spread inside him, and he died. It was so devastating because he left twenty-plus children behind.

That was a reality check for me. I quickly learned that death was real, and it was too close to me. My father's death was the very first death I experienced in the family that was dear to my heart. I was lost and broken, still trying to find my way in this world without my earthly father who was the source of financial assistance for my sisters and me. Although he was living in Haiti, he was the one paying our rent in America. Why him? Why me? Why us? Many times, we asked the why question, "Why? Why?" But there's no power or result in asking the why question; it will only keep us in the victim mode. We quickly had to make other arrangements, and instead of dwelling on the "why" we shifted our focus on what we could learn from this. And where can we go? We no longer had an earthly father to lean on and I realized that even though I made some decision that I'm not proud of, but at least I had the chance to change things around and do something different. I also realize that in God's eyes, I'm like a leper that needs cleansing. Right there on my father's funeral I made my decision and gave my life to God. I got baptized in a Baptist Church in Miami, FL.

I had to get baptized because I felt disoriented after my father's death. I was so fearful because I knew I made some decision that was not in line with God.

I read a passage in the Bible saying;

"He will wipe every tear from their eyes. There will be no more death or mourning or crying or pain, for the old order of things has passed away." ***Revelation 21:4***

And I started looking at peoples' experiences of encountering the holiness of God in the scripture and when they become acutely conscious of their sins. We see two desires that come to the foe repeatedly. One of them is the plea to be covered and so much of the work of redemption. The Bible follow the metaphor of covering.

Then I saw the first act of redemption in ***Genesis 3:21*** after Adam and Eve's sins in the garden. They became immediately conscious of their nakedness and they were ashamed that they hid themselves from the presence of God. When God came and encountered them, even though He rebuked them and place His curse upon them, nevertheless, He condescended He stooped down and He made clothes for His embarrassed creatures. He covered their shame. In that act of grace, He foreshadowed the redemption of Christ who provides a covering for our sinfulness, where we were told that all our righteousness were filthy rags. God gives us the robe of the righteousness of Christ to cover us. Even in the Day of Atonement in the Old Testament there was a covering rite, where the blood of the sacrifice was taken by the high priest in the holy of hollies and poured out on the mercy seat, the covering of the law.

But the other metaphor that is used for renewal and redemption biblically, apart from the covering motives is the cleansing motive. It's not by accident that the sacrament of the New Covenant, the sign of the New Covenant is a washing rite.

It is the bath that signifies delivered of re-generation, the cleansing from sin, because not only that sin exposes our shames, but it also soils our souls. There's the sensation of the person who has been quicken by the Holy ghost to the recognition of their sins.

I quickly had to discover my thicker skin, building my understanding muscle. I had to be strong. I no longer had an earthly father to count on. I started making better choices; going to school and starting a little-part time job as a waitress in Miami Beach. I started to like myself, not my circumstances. I started making friends with myself because somewhere down the road, I lost myself by going alone with the way I thought things were supposed to be and nothing was right for me. I thought I was in control.

I realized that I was not and still not in control. God was and still *is* in control of my life. He will continue to be in control. I find strength and hope in God and started to re-discover myself, but I think that even though I was in the process of finding myself, I was going down a side road looking for a shortcut. Eventually, I find myself lost again. My salvation was indeed intact, but it didn't mean that I would always know where I'm going.

One day I went to visit one of my older sisters. I stayed with her for a little while. She and her husband introduced me to a young guy, they meant well. He was my brother-in-law's relative. However, my destiny was already pre-destined but even I was unsure about my future. The guy was very interested, of course I was young and beautiful. He told me all the good things I wanted to, as if I was as rain to his desert, as if I was sent from Heaven right into his arms. So yes, I started dating him and once again the veil lies on my heart. Soon enough, my brother whom I was living with found out and called my mother, who was at that time living in Haiti trying to put everything back together after the death of my father. My brother told my mother that she needed to be here for her children because it takes a mother to raise a daughter and that I was making bad decisions because I was into boys. With no questions asked, my mother left her comfort zone and came over, with the hope of finding a place for me and to go back to the life she knew. Unfortunately, the two arrangements they made with family members didn't work out and that forced my mother to stay here in Florida. In a period of three weeks my mother took me and moved me to one of my cousin's house to a little town called Winter Haven, in Central Florida, because she was told that she'd be able to find job easily and the ways of living there was cheaper than Miami. She moved there with the hope of finding a job and to go back for my two younger siblings who were still under her care.

I lost touch with the guy I was dating because he didn't feel like I was worth pursuing. He came close to the area where I was living, which was only a few minutes away. He himself told me but he didn't bother to come over to see me. Well, I said to myself that he was a loser and was not worth my time. And I made a mental note not to ever let things like that happen to me again.

V. God At Work

I cried out to God asking Him, "WHO Am I? WHY AM I HERE? AND WHERE AM I GOING"? I lost a sense of my uniqueness, a sense of not belonging, feeling unwanted, and was headed for despair because I watched my life headed the opposite direction of what I've dreamed of. I was disappointed because I thought there was nothing good left in me.

I tried to ignore the issues of my life and moved along with everybody like everything was just fine, even though I was broken on the inside.

I started to go to Church more often, searching for answers I couldn't find anywhere else, because the very things I wanted in life seemed to run away from me for some reason.

I learned that God wanted me to give Him the pieces of my life that I've been hidden, and He would make something beautiful out of them. God wants me to trust Him with my brokenness. Nevertheless, when I turned to the Lord, the veil is taken away. Now the Lord is the Spirit; where the Spirit of the Lord is there is liberty. But we all - with unveiled face, beholding as in a mirror the Glory of the Lord - are being transformed into the same image from glory to glory, just as by the spirit of the Lord. If we search for God diligently, we will find Him. I came to understand that the battle is not mine, it's the Lord's. I wanted to do the right things and I needed God to use me.

Self-concept is the perception I have of me, of my worth as an individual. It is affected by how I think God values me and how I think others value me

I found my value in Genesis 1: 26,27 "God the Father, the Son, and the Holy Spirit made me in Their own image, after their own Likeness. God created me in His own image."

Self-concept and the Christian message, the message of Christianity, includes teachings which are of great importance to a positive self-concept. These teachings help me to maintain a sense of self-worth without pride, arrogance, or placing a low value upon others. My worth is determined by my origin, my condition since I was made, and the price that Jesus was willing to pay for me. God is more concerned about my future than He is about my past.

> *For I know the plans I have for you, declares the Lord, plans to prosper you and not to harm you, plans to give you hope and a future. (Jeremiah 29:11)*

My mother and I got closer to each other, we were communicating better, and I found a way to share with her some of my dreams and some of the things I struggled with. I felt a lot better because for once I shared some of the things that I was dealing with emotionally and there was no judgment. She understood!

Just when I thought I had everything under control, here comes another dilemma. Yes again, but different!

Now it's time to enroll in school in the new area. My mother had a friend who was took her to places. He took the four of us - me, my mother, my younger brother and sister to the school for enrollment. They accepted my younger brother and younger sister but did not accept me. The reason was, I was about to be eighteen with very little English. They sent me to one of the adult schools in town. Adult school! I cried my heart out because I didn't want to go to an adult school. I felt like my life was just a roller coaster. It would have been better to stay in Haiti instead of facing these disappointments. I felt like I couldn't even get a proper education. Seriously, adult school? To my understanding adult school was for the rejected, the futureless, and those who were done with life but needed to learn a few words.

> *Your best is not behind you, or before you, your best is within you*

Battle after battles, it's like I'm always fighting. Me against the world! But I kept in mind that God has a plan for my life even though I couldn't see it, but I believe He does.

So far everything I do seems like a curse. Sometimes I find myself wondering just how much I have lost because of the moments when I try to find my own way and I ended up more lost than ever.

I started praying that whatever I do next will turn out to be a blessing because I got tired of fighting things, I couldn't see nor understand. Options were few

I got enrolled in the adult school anyway. I was placed with the rejected, taking one step at a time because it seemed to me that everything, I wanted to accomplish in this life was just going against me, and how can I win if I can't see what I'm fighting against? I got a library card and started to read a lot of books, trying to educate myself. With all the wrong turns and unexpected delays, who am I becoming in life?

With all these twists and turns, perhaps I simply hadn't discovered the right direction yet.

I love psalm 23:1, it's my favorite psalm

"The Lord is my Shepherd; I lack nothing." Look it up for yourself, if not done already, it will benefit you.

I memorized it in school when I was younger.

That verse speaks hope to me. That God is and will always be with me, no matter what. I learned to take things one step at a time. I was going to school, reading a lot, learning English, working hard, and helping my mother out. I was the oldest daughter in her care, I didn't want anything to do with boys at the time. One of my cousins, who had a lot of male friends would come over often because I was there, and they would try to talk to me, but I was rejecting them repeatedly. Because of that, they plotted something against me. Lucky for me one of my cousin's son, who was about eleven years old at that time, overheard them. I was in the house by myself cooking when he came over and said that something is going down. I asked him what and he said, "they're coming for you." I said, "for me? Who's coming for me and why"? He said so and so friends are coming to get you. I was getting frustrated and asked, "What are you talking about?" He giggled and said, "You don't get it? They're coming to rape you. R A P E rape, and don't let them know I told you."

I was just standing there, speechless, didn't know what to say. I looked at him and said. "Thank you, thank you for telling me." At that time, my mother and my cousin were at work and there was no phone in the house, and I didn't have a cell phone. I quickly turned the fire off and went outside where there were people passing by until my mother got home. I told her and she told my cousin about it. They then called the boys to let them know that we knew what's going on and we are going to report them if anything happens. That's what saved me.

For that reason, my mother rented her own little house and we moved out from my cousin's house. The guy my mother was dating moved in with her.

It is funny how sometimes bad thing had to happen to push us to the best of our ability. God was in the middle of it all. My entire life, even the disobedient part of me, He never left me. For He promised that He will never leave me nor forsake me. Although at times I felt as if He did, it was never true. That was the wrong impression. The enemy was doing his best to make me feel that way. But thank God for prevailing.

> *Life is not how you view it,*
> *but how you create it*

I am so glad that what men say is not what God says for I put my hope in God alone, not in men. I have come to love these verses:

Psalm 147:11 "The Lord delights in those who fear him, who put their hope in his unfailing love."

Isaiah 40:31 "But those who hope in the Lord will renew their strength. They will soar on wings like eagles; they will run and not grow weary, they will walk and not be faint."

At the age of nineteen I met my handsome future husband, Luther. It was in January 2004 when I first laid eyes on him. He later told me that he actually saw me before our meeting because his stepbrothers were talking about me as I was the new girl in town.

One day, my stepfather was holding a little get-together at the house. He invited his two sons and he knew Luther personally and invited him over as well because he appreciated Luther as a son. It was that day that our eyes first met. Boy, I tell you, he was the deal! Handsome, stylish, and he smelled good. I didn't even have to be close to him to smell his cologne. He was different! Many other young men were trying to come close to talk to me, but not Luther. I wondered why? He showed no interest in anything else but me. Yet, he stayed far away!

I was enjoyed myself that evening and I was happy. I love writing stories, and besides writing, I love music, singing, and dancing. There was some good music playing that night. So, yes, I was having a good time dancing. Luther looked at me from a distance where his brown eyes met my brown eyes, and my precise and highly organized world rocked. It was a timeless look of recognition, of deep awareness. We were total strangers and yet we stared at each other with the look of lovers. But I remembered what had happened to me before and I wasn't the stupid, innocent girl anymore. I had learned my lesson. But there was no mistaking the sensations flooding over me, the sudden rush of excitement and the thumping heart. I'm not ready for all that, I told myself. I'd been fooled before and I was not about to let it happen again, I told myself. I was on a mission and I didn't have time to play around because I was already falling behind.

But for one strange reason, or should I say, to make things complicated, my mother kind of sensed something by the way Luther was looking at me the whole time even from a distance. Of all the young men there, my mother admired him the most. She went on and invited him back over for dinner. When he came over, we talked a little. And the next time he came over he had two little girls with him. Out of curiosity, I said they looked like you. Luther then introduced them as his daughters. My heart jumped out of my chest, as he mentioned that he was in a relationship before, but it didn't work out. And she was still alive. I had these negative thoughts rushing through my head - red flags, red flags, that's not what you've dreamed of. I stood there and then said, "Hi", to the kids. I did appreciate the fact that he was so open about the whole situation but, Dear Lord, I asked myself, "Is this another test? If it is, I'm not ready".

For one reason or the other, we became friends and exchanged numbers. He made it clear that he liked me. I was expecting him to call me the same evening, or, maybe the next day, but he didn't. On the third day, I waited, but no call came. So, I called him. When he answered the phone, the first thing I said was, "Well, since you didn't call me, I'm not going to call you anymore, bye!" He said, "No, no, wait, I wanted to call you, but I didn't want to pressure you much."

I got these feelings coming through me saying, God will do the changes when we start acting on faith, by allowing Him to be our leader. Luther started expressing the way he felt when he saw me; he said that he hasn't felt that way in a while. And I asked him, "How come?" He explained that when he and his baby mama broke up, it was such devastation that he made a promise to himself to never get into a serious relationship again. He went on to say that he would date and play around, but that's all. He said that when he met me his whole perspective changed. I shared my point of view with him on how I resented men who have past relationships that involved children, due to how I witnessed things were when I was growing up, where wives would be accused for some things and sometimes mistreated because of outside children. I said that I wanted to have somebody to grow old with. I also told him that I had dated before, which I thought was something serious but was not, and my dream was to have a family of my own, but, unfortunately, I was told that I wouldn't be able to have children due to a surgery in the past.

After sharing my point of view, I thought that would change his perspective of me. But instead, he said that he wanted to know me better. He was insisting on how much he liked me because he was interested more in my future than my past, because my past didn't have him, but my future would.

Ever since then, we've been talking and came to find out that we had a lot in common. We shared similar dreams but for some reason life was taking its best shots at us in every facet of our lives.

But when we met, we became a shoulder for each other to lean on. I was a little skeptical about the fact that his father had a similar lifestyle as my father - with many women and kids everywhere. That sounded scary to me because most boys' role model is their father. They want to be like their father if not worse, and I was not open to that. But there was a relief in my spirit when he mentioned that he didn't like his father's lifestyle, as his mother suffered great pain because of his father. His father, he said, was never married, and had many women but didn't really love them. So, he said, he wanted to break that cycle.

My heart rejoiced and sang, Hallelujah!

Sometimes the enemy tries to force our attention backward,

focusing on our past because he doesn't want us to move forward to our future. The enemy is afraid of our future and knows that he has already been defeated. He will try everything to keep us from going forward.

One-day Luther was dropping me to work. I remembered getting into his car for the very first time. His car was so clean, so cozy, and so cold. I was so nervous, and to add to my nervousness he touched my hand. I felt as if an electricity shock was running through my whole body. His touch transmitted a tingling message to every nerve in my body. When he held onto my hand, I looked at him and quickly looked away because his eyes reflected his inner power. There was a connection between us, and I felt a sense of belonging for the very first time in my life. I felt his heart, his sincerity, that he was not out to hurt me. I found that I was quivering with anticipation and fought for control.

I tried to resist him because I was disappointed once and I didn't want to be disappointed again. Disappointments make us afraid to move forward. But I also didn't want to miss the possibility that God gave me to do what he wants this time around, not what I wanted. I felt the chemistry was so strong, we were destined to be together. But I was playing hard to get! I wanted him to chase me and to demonstrate that he truly wanted to have me, that I was not just another girl to him.

He did. One day while he was at work, he called me asking if I were home? I said, "Yes, what happened"? He said he needed to talk to me. He soon came over. I rushed outside thinking that something's wrong with him. He held my hand so anxiously telling me how much he likes me and the way his heart feels when he's around me. He said," I need to know how you feel about me because I've been waiting for a while and you haven't told me anything. I know I'm not wasting my time, I know what I want." He asked, "do you like me or not"? I looked at him and said, "Of course I do. I like you very much".

I can still remember the biggest smile and relief on his face. He hugged me with a kiss on my cheek and went back to work so happy as if he just won the biggest prize in the world. I stood there thinking of how I spent years searching for a prize. There in his heart, I am the prize.

God is Awesome, just when I thought I was done. When I thought I had nothing good left to give, God sent this awesome man who wants nothing from me but pouring himself into me and refuse to take advantage of me. Later that weekend he asked to take me, my brother and sister out to a movie and my mother approved it. We went on our first date and had a great time together.

After the movie, my brother and my sister went out ahead of us and the two of us were the last people to get out of the theater. As we were walking out the hallway, he held me, and we lean against the wall and kissed me for a good minute. He looked at me after and said, "I love you."

That was the best fairy-tale moment in my life.

Two weeks later, both his mother and his sister drove forty-five minutes to come over to meet me and my family. That was a wonderful moment both to me and my family, because his mother was ill, and I thought that he would take me over to meet them but instead he had them come over to meet me. I could tell how highly he spoke of me by the way his mother and his sister greeted and appreciated me from the very first time. They took me in with open arms and I felt fortunate. His family is wonderful. His mother was the humblest person in town that everybody talked about. She was very lovely, kind and patient. We had a great afternoon together joking around like I was already part of the family.

He wrote me poem after poem explaining how he felt about me and what he wanted to accomplish in life because the minute he laid eyes on me, he knew what he wanted, and it was me. We were all into each other, crazy in love, it was the real thing, and the feeling in my heart was just amazing. I had never felt this way before.

I told him how I didn't want to know any other man than the man that I would be married to, but I failed. All I wanted and wished for was to meet that one man and to marry the love of my life and to grow old with him. "Here I am, all broken, yet you love me".

> *Don't wait for reality, create your reality.*

I told him although things might not be easy for us but with the love we have for each other, we will survive. Whether we have plenty or little, if we have each other we will overcome anything.

I remember one evening he came over to the house with his best friend and the friend's girlfriend to meet me. We sat down and talked for a long time. It was a wonderful moment and then the friends left, but he stayed. I remember I got in his car, we were talking, then we started kissing and for the first time we were all over each other and he stopped me. He held my head up and looked me straight in the eyes and told me, "We're not going to do this right now. I'm saving you". I was in complete shock, I said to myself, "Who does that"? I looked in his eyes and knew that very moment he was the man I'll be spending my life with. I had great respect for him from that very moment.

A week later I was at work, and when I got home that evening my mother told me Luther came over. I asked, what for and she said, "He asked my permission to have you, but he said he has to clean up his closet first". I looked at my mother because I didn't understand that statement. My mother broke it down to me by saying, "Cleaning his closet by getting things in order, getting rid of some stuff that may interfere with him being with you. Like old girlfriend, late night phone calls". She saw the nervousness on my face but before I could say anything, she said with a strong voice, "That's a very good thing." I glimpsed at her and smiled. She said when he told her that, she was happy because that indicated he wants to do something serious with me. Hearing that from my mother was a relief.

From then on, I knew I was ready to take on a fight greater than myself. I wanted to have him and keep him for myself. No doubt! He was my blessing.

Life has its way with us since then. I love that man so dearly. Oh dear! Did that man love me? I didn't have to tell anybody. They can already see it.

(Proverbs 16:9) In their hearts humans plan their course, but the Lord establishes their steps.

That verse finally made sense to me.

Yep, my plans were never to marry anyone who was in a relationship before and even worst if they have children. And my husband's plan was, to never get in a serious relationship after what happened to him.

In March 2004. he asked my hand in marriage. We got our parents' blessings in less than three months dating. We got married on May 17th, 2004. I was nineteen years old. It was amazing. We did it very quickly because we were in-love and we were happy. We didn't want to put a hold on happiness. In that transition, I had two different feelings, I was amazed and afraid at the same time. I was amazed at the possibilities and yet afraid of the unknown.

Did God really do this for me? Is this blessing really meant for me? I asked myself question after questions. The beauty of transition is that we get to leave some of our trouble behind and step into a new dimension.

I was amazed of the way out of my trouble but afraid of the process it will take to get there. I was amazed that God heard my prayer and finally I got the strength and the courage to make a move, but afraid of whom I would have to become to lay hold of the blessing because sometimes blessings come with persecutions.

Both my husband and l knew about each other conditions before we got married. We talked about everything; long hours together just talking. Late night phone calls just talking about things we went through and things that mattered to us, you name it. But knowing about something and having to live the reality is completely two different things.

After we got married there was this sense of belonging. The fact that both of us knew other people sexually was a great challenge in our marriage. There was a sense of jealousy, mistrust, and lots of regrets. We were both guilty and fearful. Doubting thoughts arose. Will he be satisfied with me? Will she be satisfied with me? Will we complete each other? Will we be faithful to each other? We both took the risk of damaging the destiny of our future marriage.

I personally was experiencing emotional damage that was leading to emotional despair, knowing that I took the risk of disobeying God and letting Satan get a foothold. The enemy loves it when we make mistakes, especially mistakes against God's will and against our bodies.

I was in a state of shame. That was the major weapon, and it was slicing my heart piece by piece daily. It was too hard for me to bear. I shed a lot of tears; I cried my heart out to God seeking for restoration. Its one thing to be physically hurt but being mentally hurt could last your entire life apart from God's help.

> *Pain, trial, and tribulation are the energy needed to push us to change.*

<u>Jeremiah 32:27 "I am the Lord, the God of all mankind. Is anything too hard for me?</u>

<u>John 10:10 "The thief comes only to steal and kill and destroy; I have come that they may have life, and have it to the full".</u>

We can do nothing without prayer. It will remove all obstacles, overcome every resisting force, and gain its ends in the face of invincible hindrances. CAN GOD REDEEM ANYTHING? YES, HE CAN! Take it from me, I'm a living testimony.

Did God answer my prayer? Yes, He did! No doubt. But I would tell anybody to be careful what you pray for because blessings come with persecutions. We must be prepared for all the obstacles that might come with the blessings, the tests, the challenges, the heartbreaks, the heartaches, the disappointments, the fears, the trials, the past. Especially if one is unable to leave them behind completely because of children involved. We needed God to heal us. The greatest healing is to come face to face with our condition and to seek God for help.

I think the power of the word loses its power when we put on our mask and pretend to be someone we're not. We need to realize that Jesus came to die for the very person we're hiding inside and won't allow others to see. We sometime think that God can't see it either. We often say that His strength is made perfect in our weakness, yet no one is willing to admit that they are weak. Because of our judgmental state, I think we rob ourselves from telling the truth and the truth is what will set us free. Each one must teach one another and that's how we will change the Kingdom.

My experience taught me so much about life, myself, and what others might struggle against in their journey. My story is not who I am, it doesn't define me, but instead my story strengthens me to be who I am in Christ, and as an individual.

My story is to let others know that they don't have to go through what I went through because brokenness is never a good thing to experience. I'm not proud of some of the choices I made. I wish I knew better. I would've saved myself tons of troubles and heartaches.

But I no longer give my past a power over me. I gave it all to God and He gave me His grace and a new beginning.

The reality is, we all have our own share of pains and struggles. My pains and struggles may not be your pains and struggles and yours may not be mine, but we all have them. We must refuse to be handcuffed by them. If there are opportunities to break free from them, then we wouldn't let embarrassment dictate what we let others know about us any longer.

Pain isolates us. It creates infection and when we are infected, we have these actions that we take to let others know that we are hurting, and its' only a symptom. Life hardens us and makes us feel worthless as if we have no purpose being here, but God placed a gold inside of us and as-long as we are willing to break the rock inside, we realize the many treasures He placed inside of us.

> *If you are waiting to be handed what belongs to you, you will end up in the grave with what you were born to offer.*

VI. This was me. An apple

With an apple tree stuck inside of me, without the right protection, care, treatment, and good fertilizer, I won't bloom into the beautiful tree I am meant to be.

I want to thank God for placing my husband in my path and allowing him to foresee the potential that He planted inside of me regardless of the wrong turns I took in life, and for taking the time nurturing and cultivating me on becoming the tree that I was created to be. Thank you for believing in me when I didn't believe in myself. To God be the glory!

> *The only person that can stop you from living to God's potential for your life, is the person looking right back at you in the mirror.*

This is me now. I'm an apple tree

Faith without work is dead. God is the one who break the chips, but we are the participants. We need to participate; God wants us to participate. We must vocalize these struggles, the pain, the many mistakes, the fear. That is what God wants, He doesn't want the image of perfection we put on for others.

He wants our brokenness; He loves us in our vulnerable moments and that's when the power of His Spirit can really transform our lives. We need to open and be honest. We need to allow His work to measure our lives. We need to realize that all of us are a work in progress and there's nothing that you lose that the Lord will not give you a hundredfold if you seek Him first.

We need to have a transformed mind because God is in the business of transforming minds. We need to stay positive because it's only through the Holy Spirit we will come to know the truth and when we accept the truth we will then repent.

For we now know that our conditions are not good. God has a perfect plan for sex in marriages in which husbands and wives may each minister unto the needs of the other and affirm each other's masculinity or femininity.

The story from the beginning is incredibly sex-positive. Adam and Eve started naked and Adam looked at Eve and says, "This is the bone of my bones and flesh of my flesh", meanings "This is the one." And the two were naked and knew no shame. They were completely comfortable with their bodies with each other. God told them to be fruitful and multiply. They needed sex to be fruitful and to be able to multiply, but in our society today it's hard to have a positive sexual relationship. But the story of Adam and Eve is the example of a positive, healthy, and equal sexual relationship between husband and wife.

If, per chance, one mate has been emotionally scarred by unfortunate experiences of the past, the partner has the opportunity of helping to **redeem** and **heal** his/her lover in an atmosphere of **total emotional security.** If your marriage has not been a lover's trusting place, all that can change. You can get rid of the thief that comes only to steal and kill and destroy.

For Jesus said, **"I have come that they may have life, and have it to the full,"** (John 10:10) whether you have used your life to the full or abused your life, God will take what is left and create a beautiful thing out of it, if you allow Him.

There's a song that says, **"Something beautiful, something good, all my confusion He understood. All I had to offer Him was brokenness and strife, but He made something beautiful of my life."** Bill Gaither – Something Beautiful

SEX CAN BE BEAUTIFUL. Sex is the celebration of love. God gave men and women something special and wonderful when he planned for sexual intimacy: physical, emotional and spiritual oneness. It is the celebration of love, commitment and renovation of covenant vows together as husband and wife. We need to maintain this gift in honor and purity for the purpose for which God gave it. **Thanks be to God for such a great and wonderful gift.** But unfortunately for some people, it's the other way around because of sin. What does sin do?

It separates us from God. It separates us from being husbands and wives. It separates us from our children.

Sometimes we women, especially Christian women, are facing desperate situations when it comes to find satisfying physical intimacy. Intimacy in the Christian world is hardly a verbal word, that's not Christian-like, so it's hardly spoken. But we completely forget that we are Christians because we believe in the living God, the Creator, who Himself created Adam and Eve and performed the first marriage. He told Adam to love his wife and for Eve to respect her husband. He also told them to be fruitful and multiply. God wants us, husbands and wives, to be free and to enjoy each other intimately.

Husbands and wives should be mutually happy in their intimate life and I don't mean by just being settled into a way of life. I mean to be completely satisfied from the needs of others' as lovers. This cannot and will not happen by chance or by accident. Both husband and wife need to make it happen, it's a mental kind of work. It's all a mind game. Set your mind up for whatever you want the body to do and the body will just follow.

So many times, couples don't enjoy themselves intimately because of all the negative thoughts they process in their minds towards their spouse and their body just follow their thoughts.

How you think about your spouse will determine how much you enjoy being intimate with them. To have a healthy love life, you must be in the right frame of mind towards your spouse. So, train yourself to keep positive thinking towards each other, especially if you're spending long hours away from each other. You must practice loving and admiring thoughts about your spouse every now and then. Search for whatever it is that you still find attractive in your spouse and dwell on these things. Admire one another and you will reap the benefit of a great intimacy within your marriage.

Philippians 4:8 *Finally, brothers and sisters, whatever is* *true, whatever is noble, whatever is right, whatever is pure, whatever is lovely, whatever is admirable—if anything is excellent or praiseworthy—think about such things.*

Having a thriving love life is a matter of the heart and the mind. Men and women are different and have different needs. By meeting each other's needs produces the feeling of being loved, being valued and highly appreciated. There is a great deal of what we process in our mind because the mind is the power that controls the body.

Matthew 5:28 *"But I tell you that anyone who looks at a woman lustfully has already committed adultery with her in his heart."*

> *We must take control of our mind.*

I found love in the arms of my husband, but that love came with great responsibilities, great challenges. I had dated before I met my husband and my husband was in a relationship before he met me, and he has two children I knew all about before we got married. Well, I was told that I wouldn't be able to have children, so here are my children with the man who loves me. I over-looked all situation besides our love for each other. All that matter is that I love him, and he loves me. Everything around us will work their way out.

Boy! I tell you. Did we stumble!

We were dancing tangle without knowing how to. I got into the marriage thinking that I'll be drinking milk until I graduated into eating hard meat. To my understanding all I had to do is to love my husband and try to be the best wife that I could be. NO! That was not good enough for him the minute I said, "I do." I was already a mother, or, should I say, a stepmother of two girls and an enemy of a woman that I barely even knew. (the kids' mom). That's hard meat right there because I didn't even know how to be a wife, but I also had to be a stepmother instantly and I had to deal with their mom.

For those who know before bringing a child into this world, you go through the process of being pregnant and you've gradually been prepared on how to love and care for a child during pregnancy. I didn't go through this process, I just had to adopt, and it was hard because I didn't know how to. It was not natural to me.

I felt like I was failing both my husband and the girls, and for some crazy reason, my husband had high expectations of me, like I knew stuff and I'm a very strong woman who can handle things because of the stories that he heard from both my mother and me. For that reason, he was not easy on me, and vice versa. I had this high expectation of him because I knew my husband went through some hard situations in relationships before, so I assumed he knew everything. I mean, he has two children and, to my understanding, he's a pro. Ha, ha, think again! To our surprise, neither one of us knew things. It was just a new beginning for the both of us but because of our expectations, we made things harder on each other in the marriage.

We would hold each other responsible for any little error and our favorite words to each other were, "I can't believe you do that; you should've known better," But the reality is, we didn't know any better. Or at least I didn't know better.

But neither one of us knew that until after years of so many disagreements and fights, unnecessary fights. We were blaming each other on any given occasion.

On top of that, I struggled a great deal with a sense of being second place in our marriage, like I was not in the front seat of his heart. I didn't know how to deal with that or even to address it with him.

If marriage was supposedly the foundation of the family, then as a blended family we were at a disadvantage. Why? It's because at the inception of a blended family, it's difficult to establish a relationship as the foundation.

It's clear enough that my husband's relationships with his daughters predates our marriage and are bonded by blood and family identities. On the other hand, I felt like I was just trying to feed-in and often left with the feeling that our marriage was just a secondary relationship. I was experiencing distress. Looking back now, that was a confusing situation. LOL. I mean, those were his children and they were there first, and here I come trying to be first in their father's life. I believed that I should be first.

It was a war.

But to me, that's a fair war because when I met their father, he was a single man, totally free in the market and we happened to shop in the same market. I found myself fighting to be first as a wife and the children are fighting to stay first in their father's life and because of our misunderstood marriage principle, my husband was fighting me because they are his flesh and blood and he had to protect them.

Where did that leave me? In the back seat, if you ask me. Although my husband said he loves me, I didn't feel that he does after we got married simply because I find myself in between his children and their mother. I was insecure.

I was fighting for my husband to love me and to show the children that he loves me. Another is to be accepted by them because no doubt they love their father and they wanted their father to be happy. If I'm the one who makes their father happy then I would be accepted. To my surprise both my husband and I were fighting for two different things. Him, on the other hand, was fighting not to ever allow the children to think that he loves me more than he loves them because he didn't want this kind of life for his children, growing up in separate homes. He is being not fully in control of their lives was a big disappointment for him and he felt a great deal of sympathy for his children. He was trying to protect them from stress or perhaps from feeling unloved. I felt that because of that guilt, he was cuddle and he sometimes sided with the children against me. Funny enough, neither one of us wanted to give up on each other.

The reason I say funny is because we were tempted to do so on many occasions but never found the courage to act on it. One day, my husband and I got into a huge argument while we were on our way to work. It was so bad to the point he said he was done with this marriage, and I didn't make it any better because I shouted, "I've been done with you" I just poured out my gasoline into his fire. He glimpsed at me angrily and said we're wasting our time, he's done. We're going to end everything right now. Instead of going to work that morning, he drove to the courthouse wanting to end everything. But he needed me to file for the divorce and I said no, never. I told him; he could file for it if he needed but I would not. I couldn't understand why he thought I would fill but I came to find out that most of the divorce that took place in America are filled by the woman, so to him if things cannot work out between us, or the way I would prefer, I might need out. So, he laid out the options.

But that was never an option for me. I was not accustomed to this thing called "divorce". Growing up I didn't know about divorce until I came to America and I refused to be a victim of it.

To me divorce is a disease which we give birth to through our expectations. Expectation is a killer, especially in marriages. How we think and what we believe about our spouse affects how we perceive them. What we expect and how we treat each other matters greatly.

We live in a misleading society that portrays that we can do what we want and how we want to and because of that, we tend to think that it's the same way with God. Therefore, we disregard His instructions for marriage and on how we should seek Him. That we should seek to be obedient to His words and to do His will.

We live in a society that lies to us to get what they want. They sell us things with a promise that it will work and come to find out that it's not so. And we look at God with the same eye, as if He will not keep His promises. God called us all to take Him upon His promises for He is a God who does not change, and He is not a man that He should lie.

As couple. We lie, we stumble, we fall, we make mistakes, we betray each other, we hurt each other in ways we can't even explain. But we were called to help and support each other out, not bailing out on each other especially when we are in danger by sin.

In marriage, we won't always make the right decision. We won't always have the good feelings. Love hurts sometimes but we must hold on to the commitments we made and create ways to bloom where we are planted. We can't keep lifting our roots whenever a problem arises.

We need to earn the right to stop hiding behind excuses. The truth is, we all have excuses, but we can't allow ourselves to live by them.

My husband and I moved so many mountains in our marriage and every time we did, we discovered a brighter day and find ourselves closer to God.

What are the mountains you're facing in your marriage?

And what are you willing to do about them?

> *Think positive and you will have positive results*

2 Chronicles 15:7 *"But as for you, be strong and do not give up, for your work will be rewarded."*

When we give up, we are missing-out on what God has in store for us. There are so many things that demand our attention and while it may be good to leave behind some unhealthy stuff, it's also important to keep fighting for what is right and good. Fight for our marriage, fight for our children, fight for our health. Don't give up! Understand that we are not alone, we are in the hands of God, He will provide us with strength when we need it.

At one point in my life I looked at God's rewards like punishments because his rewards were against the things I wanted. Instead of giving God thanks, I was reproaching Him with all sorts of "why"? I realized that if God had given me the life I wished for from the beginning, when I was growing up I wouldn't be humble and would not learn to appreciate the life I have now, simply because I would've thought it's my own work that got me in my position. I wouldn't give God the credit and the glory because I would think it's because I saved myself and do all the right things, is why I have a great marriage, and wonderful children. But no! I'm grateful to God because it's His grace and love that rescued me. Therefore, I look up and glorify my Savior Jesus. He is the reason for my season.

I remember one day my husband asked me, why do I love him? I looked at him and said, "I just love you." He said "I know you do. But why"? I looked at him again and I couldn't find a reason, so I told him, "My heart just loves you and I don't have a reason." He understood because he told me that he didn't have a reason too why he loved me either. All he knew is that he loves me. And if he has a reason to love me, then he could also have a reason not to love me.

1 Peter 4:8 *"Above all, love each other deeply, because love covers over a multitude of sins."*

I find myself very often thinking about the word DEEPLY in this verse. What does it mean to love each other deeply? To me, especially in a marriage, it simply means I should be able to love past what I'm able to see physically, and be able to love the person for who they are, not what they do because people do things that they have no intention doing. I should be able to love the person for who they want to become, not who they are at their present course because a seed won't always stay as a seed and we always find ourselves loving the tree but not the seed.

Ephesians 4:2 *"Be completely humble and gentle; be patient, bearing with one another in love."*

Be honest, we're writing this book because we have applied a little patience with one another and was able to hear each other a little. Not so much of the humble and gentle, but we're getting there.

1 Corinthians 13:13 *"And now these three remain: faith, hope, and love. but the greatest of these is love".*

There is no love without hope. If you say you love someone, you must hope for the best and there is no hope without faith, you must have faith of the possibility.

Don't be surprised if I tell you that the word love alone can't keep your marriage together. The reason is, the way most human love is just a feeling based on condition, and that condition comes with expectations. Okay, if you do this and act like this, and stay like that, then, I love you. But if you change like that, and you do this, and now you look like that, then I can no longer love you because I don't feel the same way I used to feel about you anymore.

Take a divorced couple, for example, who were once in love, if you were to tell them that they would be divorced now, they would have said no, never, because the love, or should I say the feelings, was so strong. However, somewhere down the line something came up in the relationship that was stronger than the love they felt for each other and the love was gone. Whether it was abuse, physical or emotional, neglect, infidelity, or finances, whatever it is, something came up that was more powerful than the love they feel for each other.

The feeling of "Love" can't save your marriage because your love for the other person doesn't make that person the right one for you and that's tough. To have a successful marriage you need the knowledge of God and you must understand God's principles for marriage, not the exchange of love. I've seen so many couples where their marriage is based on the exchange of love and they are miserable because their marriage is surviving based on condition. We need wisdom and understanding, and we must ask God for discernment.

We need to understand how to live with one another, especially our spouse. We need to understand communication skills. We need to understand how to manage emotion, how to handle anger. We need to understand the dynamics of disagreements. We need to understand how to handle unfaithfulness, broken trust. We need to understand all these things and if we don't understand these things, we're going to dump that marriage.

There are lots of marriages that could've been saved, but not too many of us have the equipment and the knowledge to use to fix the situation, so we ended up quitting because we get so tired of trying. **Hosea 4:6-7** *"My people are destroyed from lack of knowledge. Because you have rejected knowledge, I also reject you as my priests; because you have ignored the law of your God, I also will ignore your children."*

With the knowledge of God, we can help one another. God is love and we were created in His own image so therefore we have Him in us. We must be like Him, loving and compassionate towards one another.

And so often we confuse knowledge with education, but knowledge is of God is a gift from God.

PROVERBS 2:6 *"For the Lord gives wisdom; from His mouth come knowledge and understanding."*

The word of God and the wisdom of God will result in knowledge and understanding. He will grant to all who truly seek Him for the wisdom that leads to knowledge, because knowledge is God's to give and those who revere Him will receive it.

Education is acquired through the formal institution process and is of the world. In most contemporary educational systems of the world, this field deals mainly with methods of teaching in school. Education is a process of gaining knowledge for some useful application. Knowledge is related to facts, whereas education is related as learning. Education grows with age, whereas knowledge has no such growth rate, even a child can be more knowledgeable then an adult. One had to follow a system to be educated whereas knowledge can be gained without following any such systems.

One must experience the knowledge of God in order to experience true love.

And the love Jesus has for us is the **Agape** love that doesn't change no matter what we do. He is always waiting with open arms to receive us; we just need to go back to Him, and He will never reject us. That's the kind of love Jesus wants us to have in our marriages, for one another, for our children. That is also why Jesus asked us to even love our enemies, it's because if we have that **Agape** love there won't be any room for hatred or unforgiveness. That's the kind of love that's not normal for humans.

In marriage, we can't try to have any other love than the agape love for our spouse. It is the love God expects us believers to have for one another because without it our marriages won't survive. Filial love, in the concept of brotherly love, which unites believers, is unique to Christianity. We can't afford to have the **Eros** kind of love which refers to our own selfish desires, and **Storge** love is a family love and our friendship with one another.

Humanity is under attack. Our families are under attack. Our marriages are under attack. Our children are under attack and we must understand that the source of the problem is not us, it is sin. And we must not cope with our sins.

Just as unsaved men and women must come to the end of themselves in order to receive God's gracious provision of righteousness, by faith in Christ. Christian too must come to the end of themselves to find the solution, once again, at the cross of Calvary. We must turn to God for deliverance.

It's dangerous to deny the reality of our sins and our failure to live as God requires.

Our generation has been programmed to pursue happiness, affirmation and cure for our hurt feelings and damaged psyches, but God is more committed to making us holy than just making us happy.

There are those who don't learn from their mistakes, but if you find the ones who do, hold on to them because God can fix any failure. The bible says we need to forgive one another, just as God in Christ has forgiven us.

There is no room for pride in marriage because pride and promises don't work together. We can't have our pride and our promise at the same time. We should be willing to let go of our pride in order to step forward into God's promises.

> *To be a good teacher to others you must learn to be a good teacher to yourself*

We didn't want to look back but pressing forward with hope. We were on a journey and we were not leaving each other behind. Besides, a journey is always more exciting when you have someone to share the adventure with.

Changing partners is never a solution without changing minds. Unless we change our mind, it doesn't matter how many times we change partners, the problem will always be present.

The Scripture provides us with numerous examples of broken people in every case, where individuals had sinned and their difference from many of us was not so much in the nature of sin, but in their response when confronted with it. There is no brokenness where there is no openness, the greatest victories over sin and temptation is won when one is willing to humble themselves and confess their need to obey God.

Some of the most practical success-building wisdom is found in that biblical quotation stating that faith can move mountains. That if you really believe, you can move mountains. Not too many people believe that. So, as a result, they don't.

To be successful in anything in life, especially in marriage, we need to believe and learn how to approach problems and be able to make good decisions when facing difficult situations. To be good leaders we can't see things through our eyes, we must learn to see things through our mind and our belief system.

Think and believe you will win, and you will.

You can either train your mind to work for you or simply let it work against you.

There's only two ways to everything in life and God gave us the power to choose, and whatever we choose we will only see the result of our choices.

The key to understand a product is to go to the manufacturer's manual, not relying on our understanding or our opinion. To understand marriage, we must go to God. Get in the words and seek for His knowledge.

God's plan for us is to live a life of abundance and prosperity, which means a happy, healthy, and holy life. And that was His original plan for Adam and Eve.

There was this great fear and burden in our heart that whoever filed for the divorce would be the one who gave up on the marriage and would also be the one who deviates from God's plan for the marriage. Regardless of our struggles, as long there is no abuse emotionally, physically, socially, financially, and spiritually, we can always work things out, and divorce was not an option. It would only put an end to every possibility. Both of us want the possibility. We had the love, but our foundations were not established properly. There I thought about the story of the three little pigs. Most of us know that story.

(1) Where the first little pig built his house with a bundle of straw and when the wolf came, he huffed, and puffed and he blew down the first little pig's house and ate up the little pig.

(2) And the second little pig who thought that he was so smart he built his house with a bundle of furzes stick. Then along came the wolf, he puffed and huffed, and he blew down the second little pig's house and ate up the second little pig.

(3) But there goes the third little pig who built his house with a load of bricks. So when the wolf came as he did to the other little pigs, he huffed and puffed, and he huffed and he puffed, and he puffed and he huffed; but he could not blow the house down.

That's why it is so important to be careful on how and where we built our house, otherwise the enemy will come, and he will huff and puff and break our house down.

I personally think that when my husband and I built our house we built it like the third little pig with a load of bricks because God was the foundation. We faced a whole lot of challenges in the beginning of our years together, the feeling of not being accepted, not appreciated, not good enough, being placed second, with all our differences, and then when the wolf came, which is the enemy, he huffed and puffed and because of love we are still standing. Then he puffed and huffed a little harder only to discover that we were covered under God's Grace, Hallelujah, thank you Jesus! Although he tried so hard to break our marriage down, he couldn't because we belong to the Almighty, and He provides us with information that marriage is His institution.

Mark 10:9 *"Therefore what God has joined together, let no one separate."*

That includes you within the marriage as well. So, we need to know our source, we need information and understanding. We were told that when two people get married that something happens because the two now become one flesh, which to me that means one's self must die in order to adopt the concept of oneness, whenever joining any institution because where self is present, separation gives birth.

Which is why when meeting a single person their conversation evolves singularity, I. But in marriage singularity is past tense. Plurality is the present tense, we, in order to give birth to oneness. And when we fail to apply the concept of becoming one flesh, we give way to disaster in our marriage.

To understand marriage, we need the Wisdom of God to sustain us.

Psalm 37:24 *"Though he may stumble, he will not fall, for the Lord upholds him with His hand."*

He didn't promise that you will not stumble, neither did He promise that the road of marriage would be easy. But if you know that He is your source and follow the instruction given, you will know exactly what you can and cannot do.

Whatever we do, let us all do it for the glory of God because nothing good comes easy.

But He did promise us rest.

Matthew 11:28 *"Come to me, all you who are weary and burdened, and I will give you rest."*

It's amazing and sometimes funny enough when we buy a product. Notice I say buy. We cannot get a product without having to go to the source or the resource to buy the product, we make sure the product has warranty and if it doesn't come with warranty, we buy the warranty ourselves and we hold on to our receipt just in case the product doesn't function properly as we were told. We have the right to go back to the manufacture with a guaranty that they will fix the problem, because the product represents them, it's their reputation that is at risk.

I can almost imagine the disappointment in God's heart when we sought for marriage without involving Him. Some of us involve Him when we seek to enter marriage, but as soon as something is not working the way we thought it should, we seek to go elsewhere except to God, who is the manufacturer.

To get to the roots of any problem, whether in life or in marriage, you must trace the track to go back to the beginning. He who has the truth in order to find the solution. If you think that going back to the manufacturer is a long process or it will be a waste of your time, and you're trying to resolve the problem on your own or by taking short cuts with what's available around you, I can guarantee you, it will not last, and you might even destroy the little part of the marriage you have left.

When becoming a citizen in God's kingdom, we cannot keep our old ways. Every day we need to let go of the concept of self to adopt God's way. And the same apply to marriage; we cannot be in a marriage and still living with the same concept of when we were single. We must let God in and allow Him to direct our paths to a successful marriage.

God is our source and He himself provides us with His resource,

Jesus Christ our Savior, which is the word who became flesh in order to show us the way to the Father.

The secret to a successful marriage is to apply truth. And God is the truth. Get wisdom by applying the information of truth, the original information. Let us then build our marriage on the concept of information, understanding, truth, and wisdom.

When my husband and I first got married, honestly, we didn't fully have the knowledge of what we were saying to each other on the altar until we were living together. That's when we had a chance to live and prove to each other that we meant what we said. Otherwise, these would be beautiful words of entertainment. It depends on how you act and how I feel.

A PLACE BUILT BY GOD

Unless the Lord builds the house,
the builders labor in vain.
Unless the Lord watches over the city,
the guards stand watch in vain.
In vain you rise early
and stay up late,
toiling for food to eat –
for He grants sleep to those He loves.

Psalm 127: 1,2

We believe in God, we believe in love, we believe in marriage. And at one point in our marriage I was so afraid because I thought that we wouldn't be able to hold on to something that we believed in because it was too much for us to handle, but we have this hope in God

John 14:1, *"Do not let your hearts be troubled. Trust in God; trust also in me." (Jesus)*

And God knows what is best for His children because I could have had a husband without any children that didn't loved me the way my husband who has two children loves me. And I love him dearly.

Because of hope, because of prayer, and because we hold on to something we believed in, which is unconditional love and the possibility, God kept us together, and little by little our marriage was heading on a different direction.

In about three months in the marriage I had a miscarriage. I was devastated but happy at the same time because that brings me hope.

I was told that I wouldn't be able to have children and to me that was a sign that I could have children. We hold on to faith and I thanked God for giving us the strength to hold on to what He blessed us with:

OUR MARRIAGE

Jeremiah 29:11, *"For I know the plans I have for you, declares the Lord, plans to prosper you and not to harm you, plans to give you hope and a future."*

Do we still face trials and tribulation? Yes, every day! I don't think it will stop until our Savior's return, but we keep our hope in God because He is the Author and the maker of marriage, so we trust only in Him, for He is perfect, we are not, so therefore we let His perfection reflect on us. He is the only way.

2 Samuel 22:33, *"It is God who arms me with strength and makes my way secure."*

But nevertheless, due to my human nature, I was still somehow feeling hopeless and helpless and the uncertainty about our future, the doubt, the fear, jealousy, the troubled past, and the negative "Self Talk" had brought me to isolation.

A very scary place to be as married couple. It all started when my husband and I had slowly drifted apart in ways we didn't even recognize at first.

Isolation started when I started having these "feelings" that my husband wasn't hearing me and didn't want to understand. My attitude changed from caring so much to "who cares? And why even try"? I had the feeling of being unable to please or meet my husband expectations. The feeling that he was going in his own direction "a refusal to cope with what's wrong", trying to keep the peace by avoiding the conflict, is better than the pain of dealing with reality. And I was in deep isolation.

Every day in our marriage we must make choices. Those choices will result either in oneness or in isolation. If we make the right choice, we will experience love, acceptance, and the freedom of true intimacy and genuine oneness as husband and wife.

VII. The Mess We Created

I was so jealous because I didn't really know how much our commandments meant to my husband due to all the fights we had. My husband and the kids' mother share the children's responsibilities and almost every time the kids' mother called, I would get jealous because I was so insecure. Thinking that because things weren't easy for us in the marriage, I thought she wouldn't have to do much to get his attention. And besides, she's the one with his children.

There's a saying in our culture that, baby daddy never leave their baby Mamma, which I think is a curse. But that thought plays with my mind for as long as I had allowed it.

While it's good sometimes to learn one or two lessons from other people's experiences, we must also be careful on how we allow people's experience to become our future. We must understand that their outcomes are not our outcome and just because marriage didn't work for some, doesn't mean that marriage can't work.

I was in bondage by my thoughts and the things I witnessed growing up, or my thought and the things I witnessed growing up was dominating my mind to the point I withdrawn myself from my husband, the man I love, because of jealousy. I felt like he loved the other side of his life more than he loved me and I thought that he was cherishing and protecting them because that's where he has his seeds. With me my husband didn't have anything to cherish with, but just a piece of paper stating we're married. I allowed my thoughts to run with me and I got into a shell. Was that the right thing to do? No, but I did it. Our marriage suffered because of miscommunication. I didn't want to open and I couldn't stop processing the possibility of me not having my own children and the miscarriage which gave me hope of being able to conceive turns into a confirmation that I can't have children. And yes, he has two children, but they come and go and I didn't have the feeling of ownership and almost everyone in our town knows that he had the kids before we got married and when I present the kids as my kids, I can almost hear their thoughts, and the look they give could almost killed me.

I can clearly recall that one day the girls and I went to a Blockbuster store nearby to rent a movie. We were planning a movie night, and one guy in the store was flirting with me and asked, "are these your kids"? With a happy heart I answered, "yes, they're my kids". He replied, "stop lying, they are not your kids."

Okay, just kill me, seriously. I didn't fully know his motive and why he said that, but because I was so bamboozled with the thought of people judging me, I automatically took it the wrong way. But he probably meant it as a compliment at that time, the fact that I was young and was in great shape. If I were in my right state of mind, I'd probably asked him, "why did you say that?" Then he would explain. But I didn't care to ask simply because I knew my situation and my thoughts were controlling me. My husband didn't have a problem with me not having children, he was fine with it, and the fact that he loves me, to him that's all that matters. He wanted to enjoy his wife; life was good for him.

But I, on the other hand, was not fine with that. I needed a little more. The fact that I love him makes me want to have a regular family with him even more and I couldn't bear the thought that the woman that he had the children with might later become more important to him than I am because he loves his children.

We grew up in a culture that believes once you are married you should be leaning back with your belly up right after the marriage. To them that's what makes a woman. Did that bring pressure and discomforts? Yes! And children are a gift from the Lord, motherhood is a gift to mankind. In many cultures across the ages, a woman's value was based on her ability to reproduce and her worth went up even more if she gives birth to a boy. Not everyone can have children though, so it has been a source of pain and suffering for many families through the years.

Let's look back in

Genesis 11:30, "Now Sarai was childless because she was not able to conceive." Abraham's wife, Sarai (later known as Sarah), is the first woman mentioned in the bible that was barren. Interestingly, God chose her and Abraham to be the forefathers of the great nation of Israel when they were not only unable to have children, but when they were also quite old. Apparently, Sarah had accepted the fact that she wouldn't have children, and she even laughed when the Angel prophesied about her upcoming pregnancy. Nonetheless, God repaid Abraham's faithfulness by granting him a son of promise, Isaac, in his old age. So, God made the impossible possible, when He blessed Sarah and Abraham with their own son, who eventually became a patriarch of the Jewish line.

And besides, any honest consideration of marriage must think about children, the hope of our future. For millennia, people of every generation and of every culture have understood that the marriage of a man and a woman is the central pro-child social institution and the rock of the natural family.

There are so many other stories in the bible that so many of us can relate to in so many ways.

I find it very interesting that there are some things that never seem to change and the bible, which I call the family manual, has accurately recorded scenes from different eras and different families which prove this to be true. The wise man Solomon has summed it up very well.

Ecclesiastes 1:9 *"What has been will be again, what has been done will be done again; there is nothing new under the sun."*

Genesis 25:21 *"Isaac prayed to the Lord on behalf of his wife,* *because she was barren. The Lord answered his prayer, and his wife Rebekah became pregnant."*

Isaac's wife, Rebekah, was the second woman mentioned in the bible that was barren. And she was very distraught over her inability to become pregnant. As it mentions here in this verse, Isaac loved his wife very much and he prayed for her to be given a child, and the Lord grants them children. God healed her from infertility. He granted them not just with one child, but with twin sons, Esau and Jacob. Rebekah was apparently overcome with grief at her inability to conceive, but God heard her and her husband's cries and made the impossible possible again.

There are so many more stories in the bible about all kinds of lives and so many different situations.

Judges 13:3 *"The angel of the LORD appeared to her and said, "You are barren and childless, but you are going to become pregnant and give birth to a son!"*

All we need is to have faith and believe in God and He is the same God for He does not change

Malachi 3:6 *"I the Lord do not change. So you, the descendants of Jacob, are not destroyed."*

I ALLOW MY THOUGHTS TO RUN WITH ME FOR SO LONG. And I remember that God has his ultimate plans for my future, so I prayed, because these women's deliverance came after seeking God with all their heart, and God heard their prayers and then they realized that some of the things they were going through had nothing to do with them personally.

Sometimes we go through stuff so that we can realize how merciful our Heavenly father is and how He cares for our needs and to know that He is in control of it all. Some of the things we go through in life are not even about us. Sometimes as couple, we just need to hang in there and be there for each other because time has a way of helping couples work things out, by providing opportunities to reduce stress and overcome challenges

What we sometimes call trials and tribulation, God call them training and preparation because the task He has prepared for us will require strong and well experienced men and women to carry on.

We received an invitation to one of my sister's baby showers and at that time she lived three hours away from where we lived in. We did our provision and went to support her and her family. When we got there, before we could even get comfortable, one of my older sisters came and asked me right in front of my husband, "When are you going to give your husband a child?" Ouch!!! That's touchy. Is she serious? I asked myself. But I calmly told her I don't know, but God knows. She said, "Oh, I forgot, you can't have children."

She broke my helpless heart. And for the remaining time there, I was not myself. On the way back home, my husband who knew how I felt, tried to cheer me up but that didn't work because I didn't want to listen. My husband can't stand to see me unhappy. He was trying to fix the problem, which I wished he didn't because there's nothing to be fixed. I cried silently to God for answer, but God wanted to see me, not who I pretended to be. He wanted to see the little broken girl who didn't get the life she thought she needed. Yes, I was broken into pieces and was vulnerable. God took my broken pieces and started to use them for His glory.

About two weeks later I had a terrible headache, fever, and stomach pain. I thought of the situation so much I got myself sick, I was helpless. My husband took me to the hospital and they ran some tests. The doctor came back and said, "Congratulations!"

My husband looked at him confused and I said "What"?

The doctor replied, "Congratulations, you are three months pregnant".

From that moment, I knew God was working with my broken pieces. For the first time, I saw God at work. My stomach was as flat as could be. No pregnancy symptoms and I'm not just pregnant; I'm three months pregnant, which means I was already with child when my sister made her comment about me not being able to have children. God had already prepared.

VIII. Praise and Thanksgiving
Pray until something happens

W̶e Praise God for who He is. We thank God for what He has done. ELOHIM. God, the Creator and Sustainer

Isaiah 41:10, *"So do not fear, for I am with you; do not be dismayed, for I am your God. I will strengthen you and help you; I will uphold you with my righteous right hand."*

Genesis 28:15, *"I am with you and will watch over you wherever you go, and I will bring you back to this land. I will not leave you until I have done what I have promised you."*

That is a promise from the beginning of time

I knew God has a plan for me, our marriage, and our future together, and He is not about to leave us until He carry us all the way through. For His Glory.

Psalm 113:9 *"He settles the barren woman in her home, as a happy mother of children. Praise the Lord."*

This verse in the book of Psalm is one of my favorites because it describes perfectly what God is all about. He is the one who takes the negative challenges in our lives and turns them around and uses them for our good.

Besides the story of Sarah, Rebekah, and Samson's mother, we also have the story of Rachel, Jacob's wife, and the Prophet Samuel's mother, Hannah, who were also infertile. They all started out longing for a child of their own and then God blessed them with very special children. He turned their barrenness and grief into fruitfulness and joy. They had all been ''diagnosed'' as barren but God had better plans for each one of them and their offspring.

If God can do that for them, He can also do that for us, for anybody who cry out to Him for a child of their own. He did that for me. Praise the Lord!

God knows everything, and He understands. God knows our needs before we even ask, and He sees our struggles way before they appear to us. Still, He wants us to trust and believe in Him and go before him in prayer and to ask Him for the desire of our hearts according to His will, for our lives. God cares for what I care for. And one thing we need to understand for sure is that Satan doesn't discriminate, he gives everybody troubles.

Remember, God is our refuge, He is our ultimate Father and He always come through for His children

HE IS EL SHADDAI: the almighty God, He sees, He Provide, HE IS EL SHADDAI.

Trials will come, it's inevitable, and the question is, what are you willing to do? What steps are you willing to take? I suggest you go forward on your knees, not backwards. It's time for us to take actions on our knees. That's the only way we'll be able to fight the battle, the unseen battle that's going on in our minds and only on our knees. We need to have a game plan for victory because VICTORY doesn't just happen by chance, it comes to those who know their goals and move step by step to accomplish them.

Our goal is having done all to stand in the judgment, defended by our mighty Intercessor and Advocate Jesus Christ. It also helps to know the intention of the enemies so, that we can thwart his game plan.

Satan has a game plan to have our families condemned in the judgment. He leaves no stone unturned to keep us so busy with material things, the cares of this life, and running here and there, that we have no time for family prayer and studying the bible with our children. He knows that if he can divert our minds from the great issues of salvation and what Jesus is doing for us now, he will have us in his court at the end.

God's game plan for victory is just the opposite. He would have us delving daily into the family book, gaining new power as we feed daily on His word.

Man, I tell you, it was just a few months in the marriage without our own children, but because I was told that I wouldn't be able to have children, I was troubled, and those few months felt like eternity.

We must be very careful of what we allow people to put in our minds, by telling us what we can or cannot do. It's not their call because humans measure with their lengths of measurement.

They have no idea what God's measure for our lives are. And if you aren't careful, they will destroy you.

God's plan for my life have far exceeded the circumstances of my days, and the opinions of others.

I rejoice in the Lord for His marvelous Grace and Mercy, because my Savior sees me through and made my wish come true.

1 Thessalonians 5:16-18, *"Rejoice always, pray continually, give thanks in all circumstances; for this is God's will for you in Christ Jesus."*

There were no challenges, no complications throughout the pregnancy. In a few months, the doctor told us that we were going to have a baby girl. Although my husband was hoping for a baby boy, he was excited for the blessing.

I asked my husband to come up with a name. I wanted him to name our daughter and I wanted the name to be special. He came up with a first one, which I turned down because it wasn't special enough. He came up with a second one and I said no. Then he finally did a search in the bible and came up with the name Jubilee, and he told me the story and the meaning of the name. I told him, "Yes, that is it. It's beautiful and special."

God blessed us with a very beautiful baby girl and the name suited her from day one. She was the definition of celebration at the time of such an anniversary.

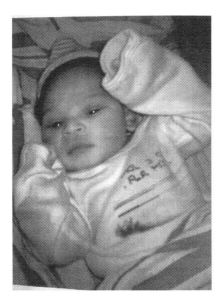

<u>Luke 1:37,</u> *"For no word from God will ever fail."*
And I, Dieuna Chrispin, is a witness. I have a testimony, I have a song, and a praise. Thanks to God.

True humility is not thinking less of you

<u>Proverbs 3:5-6,</u> *"Trust in the Lord with all your heart and lean not on your own understanding; in all your ways submit to him, and he will make your paths straight."*

I might be an ordinary person, but I know my God loves me, and He will use me to do His extraordinary plan. That's why it is always better to put our confidence and trust in the Lord, than to put our trust and confidence in man. Sometimes I find my life a very complex puzzle to complete which I can't seem to understand. Every day I wake up with an agenda trying to make sense of my purpose here.

I have so many dreams, so much to accomplish in this bright future ahead of me but I try very hard to let go and let God in, because if I don't let go of myself, God would eventually be gone whether I want to or not. I can't afford to let that happen; my whole life I depended only on God, nothing else makes sense to me. Having faith in Him had shown me many times that He is with me and my family. I was told so many times what I wouldn't be able to have or accomplish but I have accomplished them because of God, and I realized that the things I have right now are what are mostly important. GOD, FAMILY, AND FRIENDS.

God created us to be free to love Him as our Lord and Savior and He created marriage so we can experience love.

IX: Marriage. And everything that comes with it

God blessed our marriage. Our business was growing and on top of that my husband signed a new contract as a Visa Ambassador to translate English into Creole. It required him to travel to Haiti frequently for two or three days a week. I didn't like the travel part at all.

I thought to myself, "I guess that's part of the job. It's okay".

However, when it was time for my husband to take his first flight, I cried like a baby. We have never been separated from each other since we got married. The thought of me being alone with our new-born daughter scared me. It was hard. My husband and I stayed on the phone until the plane were ready to depart. He bought a phone right away when he arrived at Haiti and he called me to let me know that he landed safe.

He said, "Baby, I love you. I thought about you the whole time I was in the airplane. I even drew pictures of me and you in the future. I know how much we mean to each other."

I was so happy hearing that from him. We were in touch throughout the whole time he was away.

He had a great experience being re-united with his father and family members he hadn't seen in years.

ONE, TWO, THREE days passed, my husband was coming back home. I cooked his favorite food, made his favorite drink, and prepared the bathtub with roses for the both of us. We had a great time that evening, we talked about everything. The experience wasn't as bad as I thought until the travel became more frequent and the phone call became less frequent.

One day my husband had to travel to Costa Rica with his business partner. When my husband got there, he called me, we talked for a little over the phone. He said he'd call me later because he was getting settled. As usual we would talk quite often and especially before bedtime. For the first two days everything was fine. On the third day, I woke up waiting for my husband's phone call but there was none. I couldn't call him because he didn't have a fixed number.

"Oh, well! It's only morning, he'll call me later," I said to myself.

I waited throughout the day. No call. I looked at my daughter and wondered what happened to Daddy. I thought to myself, "Maybe he'll call me tonight."

I hoped.

I waited.

No call.

I panicked.

I spent the whole night awoke and my mind was restless with thousands of questions and doubts.

The next morning, I didn't know what to do and I remembered that my husband gave me his business partner's number from Costa Rica, so I called him. He was so happy to hear from me because he appreciates the family. He was talking and asking about our daughter. I don't even remember answering him, I just said, "Where's my husband?" He said your husband went back home since yesterday. I was really panicking thinking maybe something happened to my husband. I checked the news, no airplanes crashed so I told him I'll call him back. He said not to worry, he'll check his flight to get some information.

I called my husband's cell phone to see if he made it back in town, it went straight to voicemail. I left him a message that I was worried. Then I called the international airport, with the urgency of searching for my missing husband. I spoke to a lady, who was very nice and understanding because my English was not good. I was desperate, and she understood me. Praise God! I provided her with my husband's information and where he traveled to. She put me on hold for a minute and came back with information of a connecting flight my husband had traveled: from Costa Rica to Panama, from Panama to Haiti. Now I was curious why my husband would take a connecting flight from Costa Rica to Haiti without telling me.

I thought I knew everything. I knew he had the translating contract in Haiti, but why didn't he tell me he was going to Haiti before coming back home? Question after questions, I asked myself. But he wasn't there for me to ask him. I called his cell phone again and left him another voice message. After recording the message, the Operator would say, "To listen to the message you recorded, press one, to send the message press two, and to listen to your voicemail, please enter your password."

I know my husband's password. This was a great opportunity to hear who else left him messages. I entered the password; I heard the worried voicemail I left him and how I missed him and the next voicemail… Oh, Lord, help me!

There was this girl who left my husband a voicemail stated that she can't wait to see him, she's waiting for him, she loves him.

I couldn't believe what I heard.

My whole body dropped as if I was boneless. My body completely disconnected from my mind, my brain was swimming with millions of questions, thinking about how long it has been going on. I couldn't stop the tears failing down from my eyes. I tried to hide my brokenness from my daughter, so I hid my head on the couch as if I was praying. I fell asleep right there for the next thirty minutes. When I got up, my daughter was sitting and playing with my hair. I got up with my knees shaking thinking that was unhealthy for her.

I felt like I lost 70 pounds within a few minutes. It's been two long nights without sleep. I'm exhausted. Here I was worried about my husband, thinking that something had happened to him, while another girl was rejoicing because my husband was on a trip to see her. I couldn't bear the thoughts alone, so I called my mother asking if she were home. She said yes. I grabbed some of my stuff and headed to her house.

When I got there my mother opened the door. I greeted her and went inside with tears in my eyes. My mother asked what happened and I told her my husband were on his way to another woman in Haiti; he's cheating on me!

Laughter through my pain

My mother, oh mother! She burst out laughing. She looked at me and laughed again. Although I was in pain my mother's laughter was so contagious, she got me laughing through my tears, and I felt the burden lightened. She ran into the kitchen and brought me a glass of water.

She said, "So that's why you let go of yourself like that, because you found out that your husband is seeing another woman? You're crazy," she said.

I replied, "I didn't know he was going to Haiti, so I was worried about him, and come to find out, he went to Haiti to see another woman. I can't believe he's doing that to me."

"Go get yourself together, your daughter needs you," was all her reply.

I borrowed some of my mother's strength that day to ease some of my stress and pain. The next morning, I got up and went to a salon to get my hair and my nails done using the money my husband left me to treat myself.

One of my husband's close friends called to check on me. I told him what was going on and I gave him a message to tell my husband if he heard from him. That message got to my husband before I could even take my next breath. Guess who called while I was under the dryer? My husband.

I told him I knew what's going on and I didn't want him anymore. He can stay right where he was because I'm done with him. I guess he didn't have anything better to say besides "I hate you," and it was simply because he got caught. So, I hung up in his face. Those three words he said didn't hurt me a bit. There was nothing else left to hurt in me anymore.

I stayed at my mother's house through the night and the next day my husband book a flight back. As soon as he landed, he called my mother and he came straight to her house. He knew that's where he'd find me and his daughter. I looked at him, I fell apart with anger and bitterness, the fact that I was still in love with him. Seeing him caused me great pain because of what he did. It was so fresh in my mind as if I could taste my bitterness towards him. I didn't want to see him. He picked Jubilee up, hugging her.

I told my mother I was going to Publix because I didn't want to be there. she said, "Okay". My sister grabbed a five-gallon water container and said she's coming with me. We drove to Publix, filled the container up and we were just hanging out there killing time hoping that by the time I got back to my mother's, my husband would be gone.

My sister said to me, "Dieuna, growing up your dream was to have a husband who loves you and now that you have it, the enemy is after destroying it."

"Well, because he's a cheater"

"You didn't ask for a perfect husband."

I looked at her and said, "Are you being serious right now?"

Twenty-five minutes later when we got back to the house, my husband and my mother were still talking.

"Your husband is waiting for you to go home," said my mother.

I looked at her and said, "Home? I have no home to go to." I looked at Jubilee sitting comfortably in my husband's lap. I could tell she missed him by the way she held on to him tightly as if she knew what was going on. I glimpsed at them and thought to myself, I missed his arms around me too, but there was a bridge between us and neither one of us felt comfortable crossing.

I reached out to get Jubilee. She held on tighter to her daddy and he wrapped his arms around her saying, "She's coming with me."

I felt like he just stabbed me in the heart right where I am hurting.

"No! She's not going with you, I yelled."

I looked at my mother and said, "Please don't let him do that."

I tried to pull her away. Jubilee said, "No, mommy." I cried and ran upstairs to my sister's room and laid flat on my stomach on her bed. I felt sick to my stomach. He knew how much I loved Jubilee by my side, so he took her with the hope that I'll just come home. But home didn't feel like home to me anymore.

He called me on his way home I ignored the call. He called a second time, I angrily answered with, "WHAT DO YOU WANT?"

"I want you. I need my wife back," said my husband. He added "Can I please come back to get you?"

The only thing that was coming from my side was my tears and the loud sounds of my sorrow.

He said, "I'm sorry, I didn't mean to hurt you."

"But you did!"

"I know, I know I messed up. But I also know I love you and that will never change," he said.

"I said you have no idea what love is."

And he said, "Teach me. I'm willing to learn."

Every nice word he replied was killing me slowly. I was silent.

Then my daughter's voice came over the other side of the phone and said, "Mommy, come home." I burst out crying.

"Baby I love you, and mommy will see you tomorrow, okay sweetheart."

"Okay mommy, good night, sweet dreams, I love you."

"Good night, sweet dreams, I love you more baby."

My husband got the phone back and I yelled at him, "I can't believe you put us through this! I can never trust you again. Not only you did your dirt and now you took her away from me, I hate you! I don't ever want you again!"

I hang up the phone. I was so angry with him, I felt like I was breathing fire, my heart burned.

When something is broken, repentance alone is not enough. You need to make a choice to change and be better by making efforts and sacrifice your pride, your desires, your ego, and yourself. When these lessons are learned, conflict is simply a tool that allows us to learn about God, about ourselves and others to a place where we can grow and be a better person.

I loved my daughter so much and I didn't want to cause her pain by not being there for her because of my pain. I wanted to give her the life my mother gave me by not giving up on my father even when it was hurting her, so that I wouldn't suffer. I needed to decide where the pain is temporary for me and won't be a lifetime for my daughter. I wanted to go home so badly. I couldn't rest my mind from unanswered questions. I spent another miserable night crying myself to sleep.

"You ready to go home now?" was my mother's question the next morning.

"I don't have a home."

My mother looked at me with a smile on her face saying, "Lou loves you and he admitted that he made a mistake. Don't allow yourself to make a bigger mistake by giving up on your marriage."

"He made a mistake because I found out."

With this she said, "Well, that has some truth to it but you can't mistake your love for him. I know you love him."

I replied, "Yeah, but he doesn't love me."

"I know he does but just in case you are not too sure about his love for you right now, use your love to show him how it's done," was mother's wise response to me.

I called his sister in Orlando and told her what was happening. She couldn't believe it because she knew how much he talked about me and how much he loves me. She advised me by saying, "Dieuna, I know you feel betrayed and you are hurting right now, believe me, I know. But whatever you do, punish him, but don't leave him. I love you guys together. I see the love you both have for each other so don't make a quick decision based on your anger. I love you and I'll talk to you later."

It was fascinating how everyone knew how much we loved each other. Even my little brother, who has no idea what love was at that time, told me "Na, Lou loves you and you have a beautiful daughter who needs you."

The next day, my husband came over. I was so happy that he did because I got to hug Jubilee.

My husband said, "We need to talk, can you just come home, I promise I will not mess with you."

That evening I decided to go back home and took the guest bedroom. Yes, we have an idea of how wives and husbands could live under the same roof and yet be strangers. Listen to the same songs but dancing in different beat. Watching the same movies and yet getting different messages. We kept our routine and taking time with our daughter together. We were still working together as usual but for weeks we were just roommates.

My husband was trying so hard to win my love and trust back. The fact that my love didn't change for him, he was winning, and I wasn't losing either. So, we were winning. Our marriage was winning, our daughter was winning, my mother was winning, my brother and sister were winning, and my sister-in-law was winning. All of us were winning, only the enemy was losing.

I decided to forgive my husband not because I was weak or afraid. I forgave him because I was still in love with him, and I was not afraid to love him in his mess. I wanted to give my daughter the opportunity to grow up with her father and I felt like the choice to call it "quit" or "To perseverance," lied in my hand. My husband was not ready to let go. I had this great conviction that his betrayal was not my cue to abandon him.

X. New Chapter

As we suffer with each other, we must also learn to heal with each other. We decided to write a new chapter in our lives. Instead of calling it quits we pressed the reset button.

We danced our way through, and that one song did it for me, a song by Celine Dion, titled "The Power of Love". As the lyrics go, "We're heading for something, somewhere I've never been, sometimes I am frightened but I'm ready to learn of the power of love. Because I am your lady, and you are my man, so whenever you reach for me, I'll do all that I can."

Both my husband and I put our trust and hope in God. We lay our marriage before him and that's what kept us going, because both of us realized that neither one of us was in control, God is in control. We were ready to love like He loves.

To be a great spouse takes time and education. We read the stories in the Bible to gain new power as we feed daily on His words, growing each day to understand God's plan a little better and to see His face a little more clearly.

1 John 4:8 *"Whoever does not love does not know God, because God is love."*

Ephesians 5:33 *"However, each one of you also must love his wife as he loves himself, and the wife must respect her husband."*

It might be best for both husband and wife to read a good book together.

Marriage is a sacred thing, but it's also difficult. There are challenges and pains. But working it through and being resilient is the key to having a successful marriage.

I thought that the greatest decision I made was when I married my husband despite all the signals of things, I said I didn't want in my life. After a year and a half in the marriage, I realized that the greatest decision I made was when I forgave him after his infidelity. That decision alone was greater than myself because every cell in my body wanted to hate him with a passion because I was cold towards him. I was filled with anger and resentment. I was so angry with him not so much for what he did, because I was still in love with him and I was not done loving him because my spirit wouldn't let me leave me. That caused me to be angrier with an unforgiving attitude towards him and I thought I had the right to be angry by not forgiving his act and my sin was justified. But it wasn't, and I knew it. An unforgiving heart is sin against God and it's so great that it blocks our prayers from being heard by God.

Although I wanted to hate my husband with such a passion, I couldn't because God was at work. My husband was not in denial, he was not coping with sin, he was fighting, and he was in a war with sin itself. Instead of hating I ended-up feeling sorry for him just as much as he felt sorry for what happened. I extended forgiveness and love because I understood that it was not my responsibility to change him; my responsibility is to love him. It's not always easy to do the right things, especially if we're in the wrong place at the wrong time, we must understand our state and be willing to seek for help, and forgiveness is not a feeling, it's a choice. That decision opened a new chapter in our marriage as both of us sought forgiveness from God and from each other. God restored our marriage and brought glory to His name.

Romans 7:19 *"For I do not do the good I want to do, but the evil I do not want to do—this I keep on doing."*

Paul described a much deeper frustration, one with which all Christians can identify. The Christian's agony comes from realizing that our sinful flesh refuses to which, we as Christians despise, we find ourselves doing. Those things which we desire, we fail to accomplish.

It would have been so easy for me to just play the victim. I could say that I was good to him and did all the right things a wife should be doing. However, I know the truth and recognized my part in what happened.

Due to my past experienced, I didn't want to get hurt again. I was so hard on my husband. I had built a wall because I didn't want to be heartbroken again, but I was damaging our love for each other without knowing it. The tougher and harder I acted towards my husband, the tougher and harder he acted to prove that he was the man in the house. And I didn't understand what I was doing to myself by trying to protect my heart from him. I was playing safe but at the same time I was damaging our love because we were drifting apart. Some people build walls to keep what they have from going out there, but I had built my walls by keeping him out.

No doubt, there is no justification for what he did, but how could I crucify him without evaluating my share in the process?

I know it would have sounded so good to discuss only our victories and not our struggles, but we would only be misleading you in believing that you can win a war without engaging in battle.

There is no victory without war. No winning without struggles. No valley without a mountain.

In this life, with all the good and the evil, we must learn what to keep and what to throw away in due season. We must decide as we need to know when to hold on and when to let go.

And no matter which one we choose we must always choose to forgive.

There is a power about forgiveness that passes all understanding, especially in marriage. When your partner breaks trust with you, most of the time even he won't expect you to forgive his action. So, when you choose to forgive, you unlock something that is not normal in this world, the God kind of love, the Agape love. Even betrayal can't break that love

Forgiving my husband was not only a restoration toward him, but a restoration toward me as well. I started experiencing love on a deeper level, to the point where no matter what he says or does, I could dig deep down into my heart and find compassion towards him. I experienced freedom from anger and pain and allowed myself to move freely through life with a purpose. And that purpose was to love him with action.

I learned that through the process, if I needed to save our marriage and move forward in life, I had to act: Action to love, to talk and ask questions regardless of how uncomfortable it could or might be.

Action to give an opening ear, action to be honest about my emotion, action to forgive, action to restore, and to move forward with an open heart. Action to find peace and love freely.

At one point, I asked my husband the hardest question a wife should have to ask her husband. While we were on our way to work, I needed some closure to deal with my own imagination: "Do you love her?"

"No, love has nothing to do with it," he says!

"How long have you been seeing her?"

"Just a few weeks and we mostly talk through email."

"Are you planning on continue seeing her?"

No, never, I don't ever want to come close to losing you ever again."

"Did you have sex with her?"

He looked at me, "No, you might not believe me, but it's no, I was planning on it".

I looked at him and shook my head. "You want the truth, right?"

"Yes, I want the truth".

He said, "You know what the truth is. The truth is I messed up and now I know how much I love you because I'm willing to let go of everything to do right by you".

He broke the translating contract.

One morning a guy called him from Haiti; my husband knew him. The guy was calling for the other woman because she knew my husband is married. My husband had told her that he was married and so she didn't want to call him directly. What persuaded me that he meant what he said about doing it right with me was when my husband answered the phone and put him on speaker. He was calling because the girl was complaining that my husband never called her again.

My husband told him, "Please tell her that I almost lost my wife over that dumb decision I made. I love my wife and kids. I was lucky enough my wife decided to forgive me, and I don't want to mess it up. I don't owe the woman anything because I didn't take anything from her, so please don't call me about things like that anymore." I looked at my husband and knew that he sacrificed his desire to keep his family.

Most of us don't understand love. We confuse love with words, feelings, and emotions. Love is a choice, not a feeling because sometimes I have two or three different feelings in just one day. Imagine if my love for my husband was based on my feelings, our marriage would have been in trouble. I would run away whenever problems arise and when the feelings are not right.

One of the worst things we can do is to run away from our problems or mistakes. They will always catch up on us, so the best thing we can do is to deal with them, fix what we can, and allow God to fix the rest. We can either be a victim or a vector. We have the freedom of choice.

To be a victor, we must learn to search for the good during our struggle. We must fall upon a rock and be broken before we can be uplifted in Christ. Self must be dethroned; pride must be humbled. If we would know the glory of the spiritual Kingdom, we can be victorious.

Our story doesn't belong to us. It was the path we had to crossed in order to help someone out there.

Keep in mind while you might be praying and seeking for something that you dreamed of, a child and possibly a career, or something more, who knows, just remember to cherish and give God thanks for your current blessings.

So many times as husbands and wives, we go pursuing the things we wish to have and neglect the very things we have in our hands. We pursue everything else but our marriage. We need to keep in mind that anybody can be in a marriage, but to have a great marriage requires great work and sacrifice.

Please remember to love and enjoy each other.

> *Bloom where you are planted.*

Husbands and wives should take time to make lovemaking a joyous and special occasion. So, make it happen! Take time for each other.

There are three kinds of people: Those who **make** things happen**,** those who **watch** things happen, and those who **wonder** what will happen**.**

Now, you decide which type of people will have an exciting and complete experience in the intimate aspect of marriage.

Love is an action verb, not just a feeling. Everyday life wears away the "feel good side of marriage." Feelings like happiness will fluctuate, but real love is based on a couple's vows of commitment. "For better or for worse", when it feels good and when it doesn't.

We go through crises in our marriage, but it doesn't mean that the marriage is over. Crises are like storms: loud, scary, and dangerous. But to get through a storm you need to keep driving. A crisis is just a new beginning. It's out of pain that great people and marriages are produced.

We didn't look at our marriage like one with other choices, but to love and make the best out of our marriage, despite our struggles. Our belief is that we are married, and we are staying married, so we are pressing on by faith. We have a great marriage and we enjoy each other's company very much. There's no marriage like ours when it comes for our time together. The world does not exist. We would break up just to make up. It's worth the fight.

If there are no fights, there's no excitement.

THE MARRIAGE IS NOT A PLACE WITHOUT PROBLEMS. THERE IS NO PERFECT MARRIAGE ALTHOUGH SOME WOULD LIKE TO THINK SO.

A HAPPY MARRIAGE IS NOT A PLACE FREE OF PROBLEMS, BUT A PEACE-LOVING COUNCIL WHERE PROBLEMS ARE RESOLVED.

XI. Repentance

Relating to each other.

Sometimes as a married couple we hurt one another by our actions, the words we say, and by our non-caring attitude. Nothing brings reconciliation and peace to a marriage like a spouse saying "I'm sorry" or "I made a mistake". Those are the hardest words to pronounce.

"I MADE A MISTAKE"

No words will bring greater unity to the marriage circle. They will permit God's power to descend on the praying couple and take away alienation as nothing else can.

God informed us all not to live by what we see, yet when we see problems we panic and react to them and forget that they are temporary. When we hear them, we believe them to be true and forget that what we hear is based on what's around us, and they seize us up based on our appearance and they cancel us out as if they know what tomorrow will be. Forget that circumstances don't disqualify anyone.

We shouldn't be discouraged by the detours in life when we know our destiny. Really, if we know who we are in God and where we are going, then we will not be afraid of the challenges in our ways. No matter how many times we fail, God the manufacturer won't give up on us. Instead He wants us to give Him the product which is ourselves, our marriage, our children, and He will make us brand new.

Going back is impossible, so why not start now and press forward to make a brand new end?

We needed an instructor, a guide, a teacher because this journey will be accomplished "not by might nor by power, but by My spirit," says the Lord of Hosts. Therefore, we're asking God to instruct and guide us with His eyes and teach us every step of the way.

I am so blessed and fortunate. God favors me, and I believe that.

In less than two years, just only twenty- two months apart from having our daughter, I gave birth to a son. God just blow my mind up with how amazing and capable He is to do the impossible

Psalm 23:1 & 5 *(1) "The Lord is my shepherd; I lack nothing". (5) "You prepare a table before me in the presence of my enemies; you anoint my head with oil; my cup overflows".*

Psalm 37:4 *"Take delight in the Lord, and he will give you the desires of your heart."*

My life at this point was reflecting what I wished for and dreamt my whole life. A husband who loves me for no reason, a beautiful daughter and a handsome son, all I thought were impossible to have.

Sometimes we allow people to dictate what we should be or should not be and we allow them to make us feel like we need to have what they have in order to be good in their eyes or to fit in their world. We should know better for whatever the world offers us is temporary. This life will keep you busy if you don't know where you stand or who you believe in.

Both my husband and I realized that God was into something big in our lives and it was time to take things to the next level with God, to completely surrender our life to him for good.

We got baptized again, only this time we did it together as husband and wife with one faith, taking on a new road with God together and ever since then we never looked back. God has been using our family in such a mighty way. Nevertheless, we still face difficulties, but God is always in our mist

We realized that if we live here on earth we will have trials, but God will always give us the strength and the courage to face them all, step by step, because He is with us.

We must be intentional about our time with God and with our spouses. It's so easy to allow our busy schedule to get in the way, our work, career, hobbies, technology, and so much more.

Throughout our hard years in the marriage there was some key methods that keep our love growing regardless of our issues. We have learned some valuable lessons about love and relationship from our differences. These lessons are still crucial in our relationship and allow us to maintain our love, happiness, and harmony. And I think we were too young to understand that all storms will eventually come to pass. We didn't know at first that those times were a part of life, and that those tears would dry up in time with faith and prayers.

<u>And I truly believe that we learned and practice the universal truth that are essential for every relationship of the circumstances</u>.

1- Quality Time:

We found a way to have quality conversations rather than talking about meaningless things.

We added some fun and meaningful activities, like going out together, praying together, having lunch, traveling together.

Quality time is essential, whether you live in the same home, or in a long-distance relationship, or it may be a busy life with full-time jobs and other activities and may not be able to spend as much time as you would like to together.

Always be sure to do something funny together, do something meaningful, pay attention to each other, and express your love for each other. Go crazy on that.

If there is one thing that people know us by is that we are always together.

We could be angry with each other, but we were always together because from the first year in our marriage my husband didn't like the idea of me having a nine-to-five shift, where I would spend more time in a job than with him. So, he opened a fashion outlet store for me, while he was partner with a doctor in a chiropractor business. And when we closed the store due to lack of business, he had me join him in the chiropractor business. Ever since then, we've been working together for ourselves.

I remember one time, my husband and I had a big fight over what I don't know, but I went crazy. I mean, I was completely out of control. I packed my suitcase, I was done, I'm out.

I went to my mother's house. Oh, big mistake! I knocked on the door. My younger sister answered the door, I was crying and very upset. She gave me a big hug. She felt sorry for me and that's exactly what I wanted. I got in, my mother looked at me, and she took a good look at my suitcase and burst out laughing.

"Where's your husband?" she asked.

"Home,"

She said, "Well, why aren't you home with him? why is he not here with you?"

She knew by me coming over to her house without my husband, something was wrong, but she didn't want to hear it.

She said instead, "I'm going to call him to come get you."

I cried out, "No! Please don't. I don't want to go home."

She looked at me and asked, "Did he kick you out?"

I answered, "No."

"Did he put his hands on you?" She asked.

"No."

"Why don't you want to go home then?"

I said, "Because I don't love him anymore."

She smiled and said, "I'm no fool, I know how much you love him, and I know how much he loves you too."

I answered, "Well, I don't want to go home right now."

She then told me, "The only way you won't go home is if when I call him to come get you and he refused to."

She called him. I'm praying in my heart that he doesn't answer, or if he does answer he would refuse to get me and say so that I can go back home the same way I left, on my own.

When he answered the phone my mother said, "*Mon fills*" (my son), come get your wife."

"Yes, Mommy," was my husband's answer. It seemed as if he was already on his way.

I went into my sister's room and cried more. I laid flat on her bed, screamed like the man was going to kill me. I wanted my mother to feel pity for me. She didn't. My mother knew me. She knew I was a tough girl for anyone to deal with. Suddenly, someone knocked on the door. It was my husband.

My mother came into the room and said, "Na, (that's a little nick name she gave me) I love you too much to allow you to do that to yourself. Please listen to your Mommy, go home."

I took a deep breath. I looked at my husband with a glare that could just slice him into pieces. He's lucky I listened to my mother.

I went home that night. The next day I bought some flowers, went to my mother's house, and gave her a dozen kisses because last night was the best night ever. She saved me some trouble. I also learned a lesson.

The next night my husband and I were even happier. My husband looked me straight in the eyes and called me crazy.

Well, my only defense was, "Yes, I'm crazy! I'm crazy in love with you," and that's nothing but the truth. My husband and I have grown since then. We learned some techniques on how to use conflict as a doorway to greater intimacy.

2- Trust:

We come to understand that if we are in the relationship for the long term, we simply cannot afford to have trust issues.

In a loving relationship there is no room for doubt. We had to trust each other with a full heart knowing that we are for each other. My husband loves me as much as I love him

Trust is crucial. No ifs or buts.

3- Communication:

Communication is a key. We learned that the way we communicate with each other was key to maintaining a loving conversation. We have good intentions. We had to practice effective listening skills; to not interrupt each other, to be mindful, to remain calm and be respectful.

4- Express our love:

Expressing our love for each other was the most crucial thing in our marriage. It still is! We always tell each other how much we love one another with meaning.

Love is always the foundation. It's obvious, but sometimes we tend to forget it.

In order to remind ourselves, we would always express our love through words, actions, and even non-verbal communication. It's not a routine; it's from our hearts.

5- Small acts of kindness:

It's a very big part in any relationship. We sometime leave them behind and chase after the big deal and forget that the small one sometimes means more. It might be just a hug, a kiss, show your love with some flowers, doing the dishes, send a love text in the middle of the day, a phone call just to say, "I love you," a smile, a touch, anything to make each other's day a little better.

Your eyes will show you so much that you could get done and achieve, but you need to know your priority. Who and what is your priority? I stop trying to make sense of this life because I realize that this life was not made for me to figure out; I was made to live in it, not just to survive, but to thrive.

Now, however, how I live in it is up to me. I was created with the power to choose, so, therefore, I need to choose wisely. Life is short, it might seem long because of all the suffering, but it is very short. Put God first. Everything else will follow. I can easily live without money. I cannot live without love; I choose to love and be loved.

XII. Two Methods that kept my Husband and I together

FIRST:
<u>God</u>

We put God first. He is the center of our marriage. Apart from God we wouldn't be in a marriage anymore, at least not with each other, and we believe that. We go to God in prayer every time, asking him for understanding and wisdom, especially when life hits us, when we face trials and tribulations. When things get out of control, it doesn't matter how crazy things seems to be, once we pray, we see things differently. We get a sense of peace within that says we're not each other's enemy.

If we didn't choose God to turn to, we would have looked in all the wrong places for the solution we needed. One which we wouldn't find anywhere else to get past certain issues that were destroying our relationship. We would have lost the art of turning to each other, to talk it out in a positive way.

SECOND:
<u>Family Togetherness</u>

We spend lots of time together, but even so life has a way of taking its own turn. We had to be pro-active and intentional about not letting things just happen in our marriage and realize that if we didn't put actions into places to continue to grow our love, so many other things would have been more important, like our separate life, career, work, having a title before our name regardless of the cost. These things are real; they are happening every day in our society, where families are becoming less important, when what we do or achieve in this life becomes of more importance.

We need to wake up and see things for what they really are. On Earth, nothing is greater than our family.

Sad to say, we take better care of everything else than we do in our marriage and we look at our marriages as if it's something that will take care of itself. Hopefully, we all will be smart enough to put a little work into our marriages, where we don't take each other for granted and neglect putting the effort into continually making sure our love has life to it. We need to know that the principles for loving each other are the principles for living, as the bible lay it down for us. **_God_**, whose name means love, is teaching us how to love each other through Jesus our Savior.

We need to be willing to take advantage of what God made available to us,

1 Corinthians 13:4-8

"Love is patient, love is kind. It does not envy, it does not boast, it is not proud. It does not dishonor others, it is not self-seeking, it is not easily angered, it keeps no record of wrongs. Love does not delight in evil but rejoices with the truth. It always protects, always trusts, always hopes, always perseveres. Love never fails. But where there are prophecies, they will cease; where there are tongues, they will be stilled; where there is knowledge, it will pass away."

We need to ask God to give us endurance and encouragement with the spirit of unity among ourselves so that we, with one heart and mouth, may glorify His Holy name. As married couples, we will face many troubles in this life, as well as many blessings. I encourage all of us to dwell more on our blessings, build upon them, because in the middle of a struggling marriage, it's very easy to focus on what's wrong instead of stopping to listen to God and ask Him for guidance.

Marriage is a sacred vow between a man and a woman, and the bible offers many verses that helps guide married couples, husbands, wives, newlyweds, engaged, and those preparing for marriage.

Read verses from the Holy bible about marriage in relation to God, Jesus Christ, and the Christian Faith.

Genesis 2: 22-24/Proverbs 5:18-19/Proverbs 12:4/Proverbs 18:22/Proverbs 19:14/Proverbs 20:6-7/Proverbs 30:18-19/ Proverbs 31:10/Ephesians 5:22-33/Deuteronomy 22:5 /Matthew 19:4-6 /1 Corinthians 7:1-16Colossians 3:18-19/Hebrews 13:4-7/ Mark 10:6-9

We need to make God our binding partner, so we are a cord of three strands. We need to grow our marriage into one that reveals and reflects the heart of Christ within our marriage.

My husband once asked me, "When is enough, enough?" My answer was "Never." That was an innocent answer, but enough is never enough when you are truly committed. I explained, "As humans we need boundaries, as long as there is no abuse or neglect, never is never enough," and we watch our marriage live through that statement.

We need to keep in mind that a commitment isn't just a final type of commitment; it's a day-by-day commitment to live and grow together as couples, as God ordained. Marriage is a blessing, but we often turn it into a curse just because we don't understand the beauty of being committed.

We don't just need a partner, we need a "Life Long" companion; and the problem with our generation today is that we are not loyal. We don't keep our commitment; we don't think we can survive the odds, and we give ourselves too many choices. We need to view our marriage as one that doesn't have many choices but to make the best of the marriage we are blessed with. Too many families are drifted apart. Problems come, adversity threatens, and we don't put up a fight.

We should strive to keep the love alive within our marriage. For love we should be prepared to fight to keep something so pure and so sacred.

We need more men and women of God, who live not for themselves but to live completely for God and for His perspective of us. He has a perfect plan for us and our marriages. Let us be careful then how we live, not as unwise but as wise, making the most of every opportunity, because the days are evil. Don't be foolish and understand what the Lord's will is for our marriage to succeed.

Marriages fail when couples try to live by their own rules rather than by God's rules.

In our generation divorce has become a way of life. We no longer believe that two people God joined in marriage should stay together in the storm, trusting that the God who created and blessed the marriage will also see us through the struggles in our marriages.

But instead of going to God when facing difficulties in our marriages today, we tend to replace our spouses. The motivation of replacing marriage partners in difficulties is the hope of finding someone who will make us happy, and to meet our standards, is all about what we want, and disregard the part that difficulties in facing our marriages were not caused by one partner alone. Sometimes we just complain; we dwell on the problem and reinforce our discouragement.

Now what about the share of our difficulties we carry with us to the other side? The problem is now someone else's responsibility. Will our new partner face our share of difficulties with us? Or will he bail out on us just like we bailed out on our previous partner? Just a thought! I often hear from experienced folks that what goes around must come back around, and what goes up must come down. It doesn't matter how high it went up; it must surely come back down. We are often too selfish to see things for what they really are, until it's the other way around. If both husband and wife have this selfish, immature, me-first attitude somehow, we will certainly be disappointed with our marriage. As a couple, we really need to learn to give up the concept of self and start living for God and for others. Otherwise, we won't be able to cope with the pressures our marriage will face each day.

For example:
1. Couples with no children.
2. Couples with stepchildren.
3. No family worship, not enough time together.
4. Married but separated by distance.
5. Couples with trouble children/teenager
6. Communication problem.
7. Finance problems, love no longer expressing.
8. Couples of different beliefs
9. Couples in different Denominations.
10. Domestic violence, separation. **And so on!**

A successful marriage doesn't happen automatically. It requires hard work and self-denial in every aspect. I have often heard that marriage is a 50/50 relationship; you bring your 50% in and your partner bring his 50% in. Well, to my surprise, my husband believed otherwise. He said our marriage will be a 100/100 cause; 50/50 is for couples who holds back, who doesn't want to give their all. The 50/50 marriage is not God's way and it's not for us.

Apparently, he made a statement saying that if he brings only 50%, I should be wondering about what he is doing with the other 50%. Now let's say something happen to me, I failed to bring my 50%, what will happen if he just brings in his 50%?

Marriages cannot and will not survive on a 50/50 commitment. There's a statement that often says, "The grass is always greener on the other side," well, that could only be true if you're not maintaining your own grass, because the truth is, the grass is greener when you water it.

Two examples:

Example **1**
You, yes! I'm talking to you. Let's say in your relationship you put in 50%, which is maintaining your grass when you feel like it, because you don't care about what people say. So, you care more about holding back a little in case something happens in the future, than you do about your present. You worry more about your work because you have bills and somehow neglect your marriage, because you don't have the time and it will cost you too much to take time off from work to work on your marriage as necessary.

Example 2
Now, the other you. On the other hand, you put in 100%, which is your time, and watering your grass as needed because you care more about the way your marriage reflects your commandment as people passes by, and yes, your marriage cost you much time and money, but you care more about your marriage, more than what it cost you, so therefore you give it all you have, your very best so it could be the best.

Now, of course, anyone would look at Example **2** and envy it, but they miss the point that it must be maintain, properly in order to have a wonderful marriage. Enough said, you need to take care of your marriage and make the best of it, for it is a **B**lessing not a **B**urden

XIII. The Too Comfortable Zone

Too often, we get in the comfort zone. It's a good thing to be in a marriage and feel comfortable, but not too comfortable where we don't try anymore.

What happened to, "**I LOVE YOU?**"

I must say though, love alone cannot save your marriage, but knowledge will.

Proverbs 24:3 "By wisdom a house is built, and through understanding it is established;"

What happens to two people who were crazy in love with each other and now looking at each other as if they are roommates? They don't talk love anymore, don't check on each other as often anymore, don't even bother to ask, "How was your day"? Don't come home right after work anymore, and when you're finally home you would rather find things to keep you busy so you don't have to interact with your mate, and when its bed time, you rather sit in front of the TV falling in and out of sleep instead of coming to bed while your partner is still awake. When you finally get to the point where you really want to lay down to be more comfortable, you take the next room to be alone, and next morning when you get up your partner looks for you, and you are nowhere to be found, you have already gone to work without a good-bye kiss. Even a "See you later," would have been fine at this point, but they get none, you completely stopped trying. Please, don't allow your marriage to get to the point where you are too comfortable. It's unsafe, because it's cold even though its 90 degrees there.

Give a little, try harder, and it will get better.

Aim for greatness so in case you miss, you will at least fall in the good category. But imagine if you settle for less what category will you end up with?

Sometimes our efforts seem small because so many forces tear families apart today. The odds seem stacked against us. We might feel like we don't have the resources to meet the great problems that burden us. But we must remember that God is eager to multiply our efforts. When we act in faith, He responds and magnifies those actions. His strength made perfect in us.

My husband and I face challenges in our marriage but our commitment to each other remains on top. I love my husband and I know my husband loves me, so we must pray and rise above our circumstances. Sometimes we ask God to give us a praise during our sufferings and situations. To be an effective prayer we must be an effective lover, Jesus loves of my soul. Let us sing love songs to our Jesus. Our Jesus is love and if we are from Him, we should love one another.

When we look back at our lives, we realized that those people that crossed our path and the struggles we went through were just stumbling blocks that God had to remove so that we can come to see His glory. We must give Him praise.

Marriage is regulated by God's commend. God creates marriage and He gives it to us as a gift. God institutes marriage. Marriage is a covenant. What is a covenant, one may ask?

A covenant is simply an agreement, a contract between two or more persons, and at the heart of a covenant is a promise. In biblical terms, every covenant has stipulations, it has provisions and rules, if you will, that must be kept for the covenant to stay intact. A covenant is not a private matter, a covenant is something that is undertaken in the presence of witnesses. The covenant is before God, parents, families, pastor, friends, church family and so on. You make a promise, you take vows, sacred vows, holy vows and you make a commitment that if you don't take it seriously maybe your parents or your friends, and you have all these people holding you accountable for your marriage. We often think that if we end a marriage, we're not affecting anybody else but the two persons in the marriage, that is not true.

I often hear others say, "Well, I'm not happy, and if I stay in the marriage, I'm only hurting myself." Without thinking or seeking for help, they just want to check out without thinking that if they end the marriage, they will hurt tons of other people; the one they once said they loved. Their own children, and many others. They think it's only between two persons, but it is not so.

Happiness in a marriage is by choice, not by chance.

We need to make a choice to trust God and learn to focus on the possibility it holds for tomorrow and not just on the NOW. Yes, your "now" moment might sting, but who knows what tomorrow might be.

If only we know the outcome of things, we would try a little harder, be a little more patient with each other, love a little deeper, play with each other more, laugh together, be easy on each other, have less conflict, and make more love, communicate more effectively, express gratitude, treat each other with respect, admire each other in public, ask each other and don't demand, prioritize your partner. Focus on building experiences, complete each other, and don't compete with one another.

We need to know that people's experiences are not God's will for us. And when we know God's will for us, then we will not be discouraged by the detours of life because we know our destiny.

If you know who you are and where you are going, then you will not be afraid of the challenges in your way because true love conquers evil.

Submission attracts responsibility. If you submit completely to God, then He is responsible for you.

Luther and I didn't have much to offer each other, but words of promise to stick by each other's side, to love and cherish each other, through the good and bad times.

Yes, we have an idea of what good and bad times feel and look like by now.

When we got married, we couldn't afford to get our own house, so I moved with my husband into his one-bedroom apartment, where we lived for a short period of time. Then we moved to our first three-bedroom house that we rented together in Kissimmee, Florida where our daughter, Jubilee, was born. We stayed there for two years, and we moved again, yet in the same area but this time to a two-story house with four bedrooms, which was almost the same price we were paying for the three-bedroom house. We stayed there for almost two years and then were ready to buy our first home together. We found our dream home in Cypress Garden, Florida, with everything we wanted. Nice neighborhood, pool, jacuzzi, large backyard, you name it. We were settled. Then our son Luther II was born.

We committed ourselves to God and we were on a mission for Him. He was using us left and right, and we knew we were on a different track of our lives when we started losing friends because of our commitment to serve God. But nobody understood, we needed to survive, and God was our only answer. Because people didn't see us as broken, they felt like we were doing great in our path and so decided to change.

Like they say, if it's not broken, why fix it. Well? I say some breakage is just not visible for others to see. I thank God that both my husband and I were not in denial that we needed a deeper help from above. We went for it with full speed and never looked back.

We served God in our local church in Winter Haven.

I can clearly recall a couple of times going to church, when we were arguing about our issues, up to the church parking lot, but the moment we made it into the sanctuary, there was this feeling of peace flowing within me, and we would hear a message, and my husband would stare at me, and sometimes I didn't even want to look at him. He would whisper in my ear, "I love you," and wrapped his arm around me, and I felt safe once again.

One Friday, there was a marriage seminar in the church by the Family Life Ministry. My husband and I went to the seminar and when we got there, as a warm-up they were having this game of who knows their spouse better.

I knew my husband and I know a whole lot about each other because we spent lots of time talking about our wants, our needs and about our future. But I wasn't sure if we were ready to get in a challenge with couples who have been in a marriage for over twenty years. We were only married for four years at that time, but we were encouraged to participate, so we took on the challenge. Surprisingly, my husband and I won as the couple who knew more about each other and our prize was the book "TO HAVE AND TO HOLD: A Guide to Successful Marriage," by Nancy Van Pelt. I was amazed!

To my surprise, as if God wanted to assure my insecurity about my marriage in the future, our pastor at that time made a comment that spoke directly to my heart, by saying, "If you forgive a husband who loves you but committed adultery against you, you will have the most committed husband for life. People fall because of sin, and when they find true forgiveness, it's speaks volume to them."

I said to myself, our journey might be rough and tough, but we will reach our destination, till death do us part.

Well, that was our hometown for five years until we had a different vision for our children and our spiritual life. We were on a quest and God was on a mission.

We were planning to move somewhere far away from Florida, but in January 2011 we found ourselves in West Palm Beach, Florida. Life didn't turn around exactly the way we planned. After all, life happens. We had to adjust, we had to make plan B, and even, a plan C at that point.

We watched ourselves go from having our own dream home to

renting a little apartment just to make ends meet, from owning the top Cadillac truck of the year, to walking to Walmart to buy our daily groceries. From eating at a top restaurant, to eating noodles because that's what we could afford. From having it all, to just trying to survive. We left our used car dealership back in Winter Haven in the care of my brother-in-law and hoping to open a branch here in West Palm Beach. That didn't happen, so my husband had to travel back and forth from West Palm Beach to Winter Haven three to four times a week for two years, buying and selling cars at the dealer's. That was our only source of income.

It was hard to find a job, so everywhere I applied for a job. I was turned down. Besides that, I hadn't work for other people in years. Our daughter was five, going on six, and our son was about three years old. Wonderful children, just a glimpse at them could give you a reason to smile and know that everything's going to be all right.

There were tiring nights of driving where my husband could've slept at his brother's house because the next morning, he had to drive up there again. Each night, I watched my husband made sacrifices to come home because the kids were waiting for him. My daughter would tell him, "Daddy, I'm going to stay up until you came home and if I fall asleep before you came, please wake me up." And that was my husband's boost every night.

I saw how the whole process was weighing him down and as much as I didn't want to anticipate the thought of him staying up there, I gave him that choice of staying at his brother's or his uncle's and come back the day he wouldn't have to go the next morning. He refused because the kids were expecting to see him. He thought that was the right thing to do.

I went to a workforce to get help creating a resume and they told me about an Edison Publishing Company that was looking for agents. I signed up and was scheduled to take the training and be tested. I did well and was given two weeks to prove my ability in pitching sales, including opening, reporting and the closing process of a sale.

I was on top of the world when I closed my first sale in three day. I got a commission and I felt good, but not so good because my schedule wasn't going well with the time with the kids' school. For some reason, my two-week period was approaching, and I couldn't close another sale. They had to let me go. I called my husband with great disappointment because I was so close, but now I'm back to looking for a job again. Only this time, I'm focusing on finding a job with a more flexible schedule around the kids' schedule, because my husband's hands were already tied. I did a research online, found a daycare that was hiring, and I thought to myself, "That could be a good choice where I can have the kids with me in aftercare at the daycare."

I looked to see what the requirement was to work in a daycare facility. First step, I needed a forty-hour of childcare training. I got my forty-hours of training and was ready to work. The first daycare I applied for, I was interviewed and got the job on the spot. While I was working there, I was inspired to do more because caring for children is my passion. I had this great idea of opening my own family daycare and shared the idea with my husband "It sounds good," he said. On the other hand, my husband was in the process of getting a dealer's license here in West Palm.

I gathered some information about the family daycare. They have tons of rules and regulations. I called zoning, the house was zoned so I called all the other departments and applied for the license. I quit the daycare job, which everyone thought I was crazy for doing so, but I had to take that other step into my vision. For some reason, it took longer than I expected to get the license. My husband got the dealer's license, so we were back on working together again and after a long year waiting, we finally got everything together and the government approved the daycare license on February 11th.

God blessed the daycare. Before I knew it, I was telling parents that I was full and have no opening spot. Now I'm in the process of opening a facility. Praise God.

Talking about perseverance and being consistent when believing in something is no joke. It is hard work and dedication, with a positive attitude. Now I have more time with my family and can work towards my writing dream.

We had a taste of our own words, which I believe is every married couple's words, right on the altar. We Vowed!

XIV. For Better Or For Worse

$\mathbf{A}$nd we're lying, right there on the altar, before God, our spouse to be, our pastor, our parents, our families, friends, and sometimes our children because we have no idea what worse is, or would be in a marriage, and for most of us we **thought,** or at least **wished** that **WORSE** would simply mean **IF** but not **WHEN.**

I wish all couples would be told that it's not a question of **IF.** They'll face serious challenges in the marriage, but it's a question of **WHEN.** Then they would be better prepared to adapt to change, and to let go and let God, because there are things that simply cannot be controlled by either one of them.

But we thank God because we got stronger. Our love has grown and endured much but we're still in the race, it's not over yet. We're still students of the kind of love that will last and will keep burning long and bright into the unknown future ahead of us.

Not easily broken, is what God creates in us.

And the "for BETTER" part, is the ice on the cake, where we help each other be better people in reaching spiritual and personal goals. We are for each other.

Some of us sometimes allow our past hurts to keep us from taking chances with love again. What happened between Luther and I was that we traded our hurts with God for healing and He gave us love in our marriage for the healing process to take place, where we come to know the power of His love.

God is the foundation of our marriage. Neither my husband nor

I were relaying on what we saw or knew, we just took a leap of faith based on what God placed inside of us, a dream and a true love for one another.

> ## *A gift or belief can't be defeated*

The more you improve your relationship, the better you improve your life. I don't have time to spend the rest of my life wondering how things should've been or could've been for me and my children. The world has enough of that already. I made my choice not to allow myself or my children to be a victim of the environment, but to seek knowledge from the source.

> ## *Humbly seek God's grace to overcome sin.*

We Christians need to continually view ourselves as needy recipients of God's grace, not dispensers of self-made virtue. He gives more grace. Therefore, it says. "God opposes the proud but gives grace to the humble.

James 4:10 ' *Humble yourselves before the Lord, and He will lift you up."*

Trust God to work on each other's lives; there is only one Lawgiver and Judge, the One who can save and destroy. We must seek daily to have a pure and forgiving heart. It is crucial that we forgive each other. We cannot receive forgiveness if we're not willing to release forgiveness ourselves.

Jesus Himself tells us, "If we forgive men when they sin against us, our heavenly Father will also forgive our sins."

I loved my husband, so I decided not to leave my marriage up to my feelings. I made a choice to live for today and leave the tomorrows into God's hand because sometimes we refuse to move forward with those who failed us, not because we don't love them anymore, but because we are afraid of the possibility of them failing us again in the future. We rather get rid of them instead of giving ourselves a chance to see what tomorrow will bring, we let go based on assumption. A lot of married couples ends up in divorce and live in regrets for the rest of their lives.

My husband loves me and was willing for whatever. We were willing to take each other on this journey, with a very different approach and state of mind.

<u>We didn't just want to be in a marriage. We wanted our marriage to thrive.</u>

We hold on to each other and believe that together we can climb any mountain and we strongly believe that God wants us to move every mountain that comes our way, for His glory, with a promise that He will be with us always.

<u>**Galatians 6:9**</u> *"Let us not become weary in doing good, for at the proper time we will reap a harvest if we do not give up."*

God has set us free; we are no longer under the bondage of sin, we are no longer live under the bondage of our past. We find hope in our Lord Jesus Christ.

I love my husband for the person that the world doesn't see, for his innermost being. We sometimes fail to accept one another based on the person's condition, his/her circumstances, and fail to get to know him/her. We assume that we know the person based on what has happened and most of the time, we are wrong.

Luther and I saw something in each other that no color, no race, no height, no size, no brokenness could take away from us. Our belief and faith in God cause us to refuse to allow our background and circumstances to define who we are and who we are becoming.

Powerful couple is what we call ourselves.

> *Courage is doing the things*
> *life dares you to do*

This is a picture of our tenth-year Anniversary

We are two separate individuals, unique and whole and we both bring our different flavor into the marriage. And as you can see, we still have many stairs to climb and we will climb them all the way through together. Attraction may have sparked interest, but our relationship was built on a bond that took time to build.

There is no such thing as a perfect marriage, everybody fights and struggles to make it.

It's just that some people put their trust in God more and work harder than others, simply because they have faith that things will get better for them somehow. That's all! It's faith.

And it's never based on how we start, it will only be based on how we finish. It's okay if we stumble, but it's important to reach the finish line.

Choose your battle, fight fair, fight a good fight. Every problem in our marriage was an opportunity. When things get hard for us, we would be frustrated, wouldn't know how to act, and wouldn't even know how to address each other properly. We talk at each other instead of talking to one another. We take it upon each other.

Instead of putting ourselves together to solve the problem, we divide ourselves because we both have our own standards of how things should be. We have our own rules and principles and we won't break them for anybody, and we forget that we joined each other to become one.

Lifelong commitment: Thriving couples highly value their marriages. They are committed to devotion, loyalty, fidelity, and hope. We have a deep conviction that divorce was not an option. We are committed to a shared purpose and dream of a positive future together.

PSALM 5:1-3, *"Listen to my words, Lord, consider my lament. Hear my cry for help, my King and my God, for to you I pray. In the morning, Lord, you hear my voice; in the morning I lay my requests before you and wait expectantly."*

Each day we ask God to give us wisdom, wisdom to choose to do what is right. So often we know the right things, but we choose not to do it just because it's not convenient for us. We pray for wisdom to thrive to be a better person, not in our own eyes, but so that others will see that we are better in Christ.

A better servant of God, a better wife, a better husband, a better mother, a better father, a better person through our Lord Jesus Christ.

Many of us sometimes struggle with a sense of our lives' purpose. I know that God created each one of us for a reason and it is our responsibility to go to Him in prayer and ask that He reveal Himself to us, so that we could fulfill His will for our lives.

So often we become lost in the maze of our own mistakes. We became so stubborn and refuse to ask for directions, when God is right there waiting.

So often, we don't reach our full potential in life because we go in our own direction instead of trusting God to guides us. We learn some hard lessons and we're still a work in progress.

XV. Our Commandment

I will seek, with my spouse, to teach the next generation the truth of God's word as they relate to all of life.

We will maximize the influence of our marriage, which will outlive us and display the works of God to coming generations. The legacy we have received is not as important as the legacy we will leave.

Thank you, Lord, for giving me my spouse, crafted for me. I trust your perfect love for both of us, as well as your knowledge of what we truly need.

Give us perseverance, courage, and the desire to love each other as you love us, let our love and our marriage and its legacy be a lasting reflection of who you are.

OUR HEART REJOICES IN THE LORD.

A marriage worth fighting for

God is our perfect Father, shepherding us toward grace and truth. He is our model and He is our source. We need patience, truth, wisdom, grace, love, and peace to encourage each other in this journey.

Jesus is the vine, we are the branches. Stay connected!

Love is a gift, cherish it!

Your relationship is like a tender plant, it needs to be nurtured. Don't take things too seriously all the time. Take some time to laugh together. Spend time together talking about dreams, goals, and ideas. Show that you care. Don't forget to invest 100% in your relationship because we can only reap what we've sown.

And don't be too quick to give up.

Take time to work through the difficulties.

Forgive and forget.

Admit your mistakes and ask for forgiveness.

The greatest gifts and the greatest riches in this world is family.

XVI. Serenity Prayer

God grant us the serenity to accept the things we cannot change; the courage to change the things we can; and the wisdom to know the difference. Teach us to live one day at a time; enjoying one moment at a time; accepting hardships as the pathway to peace; taking as He did. This sinful world as it is, not as we would have it; trusting that He will make all things right if we surrender to His will; that we may be reasonably happy in this life and supremely happy with Him forever in the next. AMEN.

-Reinhold Niebuhr

> *Not to us, o Lord, not to us, but to your Name be the glory, because of your love and your faithfulness. Psalms 115:1*

If you come from a broken past and you are still healing from the scars, **the best is yet to come**.

If you are on top of the world today, if are finding fulfillment in your family, your health is good, you are doing well in your job, **the best is yet to come.**

If you are going through a heart-wrenching agony and trauma of divorce, and you are wondering how to pick up the pieces of your life, **the best is yet to come**.

If some sin has a hold on you, and imprisoned you, **the best is yet to come.**

Fear tends to blame God for the problem, but **Faith** trusts God through the problem.

The grace of Christ is greater than all failures.

May God bless and keep you, and may you find strength in JESUS CHRIST.

XVII. Letter to Wives:
Dieuna P. Chrispin

Proverbs 7:15-16 *"So I came out to meet you; I looked for you and have found you! I have covered my bed with colored linens from Egypt."*

Not too many things are more abhorrent to us wives than seeing women make sexual advances toward our men or any married men, either on TV or in real life. We recoil at this kind of behavior. But again, just because flirtation is often corrupted don't mean that there's anything wrong with making sexual advances toward the one, you're already married to.

The power of a woman:

This includes all women, single or married, but we often act as if it's only the single woman with the power because marriage happened, and forget that you were once a single woman and you can recall all the good things you did that caused him to want to keep you around and to even want to have you for himself.

A single woman is aggressive because she wants to be in your position, so she'll do whatever it takes.

But you, who are there, what are you willing to do to maintain your position?

There are some passages in the bible that sometimes raise a question in my mind like, "Why are they there especially if it's against God's law?" I believe all passages are there for a good reason and there is always a lesson to learn from them. Let's look at:

(Proverbs 5-7) "And I believe we can learn something from the powerful woman in these passages. Although she is an adulteress and would not typically seen as a positive role model, perhaps there is a pure use of this power when these tactics are directed toward a woman's own husband."

For example:

Proverbs 5:3. *"For the lips of the adulterous woman drip honey, and her speech is smoother than oil."*

There was a time during the dating season when gentle, smoothing speech came easily, but now in marriage, it's all too easy to gripe and complain. Words are powerful. Use yours well and you'll melt him like butter.

"She took hold of him and kissed him" (Proverbs 7:13). Can you imagine the look on your husband's face if, when you first see him at the end of a day, you grab him around the shoulder and really planted a kiss on him? There's not a husband on planet earth that wouldn't love that.

"Do not lust in your heart after her beauty or let her captivate you with her eyes" **(Proverbs 6:25).**

We wives tend to get sloppy with our appearance around the house. That's understandable. But every now and then, make sure you look good when he comes home, "REALLY GOOD." Use your eyes to capture him with your physical attractiveness.

A wife who understands her allure as a woman is protecting her husband from temptation. She's like a magnet, drawing him home from the seduction of his long day.

She's got power and she knows' how to use it in her marriage.

Proverbs 31:10-12 *"A wife of noble character who can find? She is worth far more than rubies. Her husband has full confidence in her and lack nothing of value. She brings him good, not harm, all the days of her life.*

What a husband wants?
Simple: **Respect.**

That means a man wants to be held in esteem and to be shown

consideration and appreciation, even when he makes mistakes. He wants to be a hero, especially in the eyes of his wife.

I, myself, as a wife, learned that in the beginning of my marriage through tears I love and respect my husband with my whole heart. My attitude says otherwise, and my husband would look at me with great disappointment in his eyes and would say, "You don't respect me." That broke my heart to hear him say that. I used to scream, "I respect you," but the way I talked to him, the way I looked at him, the way I doubted his choices, showed him otherwise. And because I respect him, I wanted him to feel it, so I learned over the years how to show him respect even when I don't say a word.

He needs his bride to believe in him when the odds are against him, and men don't believe that they should earn respect as some wife feels like they should earn respect. They feel it is owed to them simply because they are men. God told us wives to respect our husband, period. Not respect them when they earn it. It is so important for a woman to learn to give her man unconditional respect. Not only you are obeying God, you are also winning your husband's heart.

A man needs respect to feel safe enough to open-up. When he feels he's being looked up to as the head in the relationship, he will automatically allow his wife to become the "neck" and she will be able to point her man in the right direction. As wives, we have the power to build up or tear down. The choice is yours.

Living in gratitude for the things you already have is the first step to happiness. This goes for everything, physical, spiritual, and mental in a relationship.

Most of us struggle with life simply because we haven't paid the price to decide what's important to us.

There is never anything but the present and if we cannot live there, then we cannot live anywhere. We must accept to live in the present in order to move to the future together.

Be a great student of your journey

Letter to Husbands: Luther K. Chrispin

Genesis 2:23 *"The man said, "This is now bone of my bones and flesh of my flesh; she shall be called 'woman, for she was taken out of man."*

Mark 10:8 *"And the two will become one flesh. So, they are no longer two, but one."*

Proverbs 18:22 *"He who finds a wife finds what is good and receives favor from the Lord."*

Almost all men know how to find and pursue a woman before marriage but by continuing to pursue and love your woman even after marriage and not being harsh with her, you are showing love. Love is a verb – it's an action, it's what you do. Saying "I love you" is important, but showing it with loving kindness, consideration, and a soft-spoken tone is more important than you can scream, "I love you." A tender, soft kiss tells your wife more than a hundred, "I love you," ever could.

Ephesians 5:25 *"Husbands, love your wives, just as Christ loved the church and gave Himself up for her."*

Wives are not a law of physics, but rather a puzzle, one that resists being pieced together, solved, and framed on the wall.

WHEN A MAN LOVES A WOMAN, a woman has a few basic needs that a man must learn to meet if he desires to love her as God intended.

A spiritual leader: A woman long to follow a man of courage, conviction, commitment, compassion, and character, to be a capable and competent student of the word of God.

God intended marriage to be wonderfully enjoyed. He wants it to be a blessing. For us to experience maximum marriage satisfaction, it is essential that we grow to know each other.

Romance. Romance for us men is sex. We cannot imagine romance without having sex. But romance for a woman can mean lots of things and sex may or may not be part of it.

Romance is basically a game. It is a specific game. It is a game of "hide-and-you-go-seek." She hides it and you seek it. If you find it, you will indeed agree that it's good! On the other hand, if you don't find it, you have two options: First, you can get angry and be bent out of shape. Second, you can remind yourself that it's a game, sometimes I win and sometimes I lose, but that's the fun of the game.

Solomon encourages husbands to "enjoy life with your wife, whom you love." Enjoy your time with your wife, sacrifice a football game to go to an event that she enjoys, she might remember the days before you got married that you went to the park with her, took long walks in the evening, spent late nights talking your future together. We should redeem that time with our wives because time flies and who knows, these things might be romance to your partner.

Honesty A woman needs a man who will consider her eyes with love and explain his plans and actions clearly and completely to her because he regards himself as responsible for her. He wants her to trust him and feel secure.

Security. A man who loves a woman will firmly shoulder the responsibilities of the family, he will provide and protect. There will be no doubt as to where his devotion and commitments lie. They are with his wife and children.

Intimate conversations. A woman needs a husband who will talk with her at an emotional level (heart to heart). She needs a man who will listen to her thoughts and talk about the events of her day with sensitivity, interest, and concern.

Family commitment. A woman longs to know that her man puts the family first. Such a man will commit his time and energy to the spiritual, moral, and intellectual development of the entire family. She needs a man who puts his wife and children right after his commitment to the Lord Jesus Christ.

When a husband is committed in this way, and when the wife has the same commitment, it is not surprising that both husband and wife have smiles on their faces and joy in their hearts. This is the way God intended it from the beginning, so settle for nothing less.

Life is a journey from the time we were born to the point of death. It's a journey we all must take, long or short. It's a very exciting journey for those who are willing to face the unknown and are willing to discover the joys and sorrows, the ups and downs, the good and the bad, the fun-filled day and the sad lonely nights, the hills and the valleys, the calm and the storm, and everything else the journey of life brings with it. When we reflect on lessons learned from the lives of those before us, we cherish some and wish others would vanish, but they all work together to reveal that lives of great men and women were not a walk in the park, but a strong determined effort to climb rugged mountains, navigate slippery roads, make bold decisions at every critical crossroad, and all the time making an inward resolve that they would push through their destination.

> *Consistency is a major key*
> *to achieving something*

LETTER TO SINGLES BY: Luther and Dieuna Chrispin

Being single and yet complete.

Singleness is beautiful and is a gift. Being single can be an important stage in life that comes with many benefits. Being single is an opportunity to be whole in God First and Foremost. Then when you get in a relationship with others, you will be an asset to that person rather than a liability. A great marriage is made up of two complete singles, and one of the reasons why marriages are failing today is because the people in the marriage were never complete men and women in the first place before they got married to each other. They never really knew God's purpose for their lives. They grew up thinking that marriage will give them the fulfillment they need instead of God. The only person you can't afford to live without is God. If single people get into marriage with the mentality of finding fulfillment through another human being, you will be greatly disappointed because such burden on man or woman, to give you fulfillment will strain whatever marriage you go into. Singleness is a season of preparation where God molds you and shapes you for what and where He wants to take you.

Like Paul said, "It's a time that you can use to throw yourself into God and His plan for you with no distractions."

And when you allow God to prepare you through your singleness, by the time He finishes with you, you will be a complete asset to anyone who walks into your life, not a deficit. Don't let circumstances take your praises to God out of your mouth. He knows you, He cares for you and He never miss anything, so rest in His assurance. It is better to be single and happy than to be married and depressed. Single people, please don't depend on marriage to bring you happiness. Don't look to someone else for your emotional and financial resources. Being single does not mean you are alone.

It is funny when we meet single people who think that they are lonely because they are single, and yet we also know of married couples who are lonely. It is okay to be single but it's not good to be alone. Your singleness will determine the quality of your marriage. You are only as good as your single life so focus on developing yourself, focus on refining yourself, focus on making yourself more valuable as to be a blessing to someone in the future, not a burden.

> *May God bless you and use*
> *you on your journey*

XVIII. A Trip To Freedom It Is Important To Talk With God.

The path to freedom is the cross through prayer. It is very important to have a close relationship with our heavenly Father, our Creator. Pray and seek God for freedom from strongholds.

Begin by *praising God in worship*: Praise Him because of who He is and what He has done for us.

Confession: get the junk that is unlike our Savior out of our life through the Holy Spirit who is revealing the truth to us.

Read the word of God: God's word helps us see ourselves as in a mirror, and it also helps us to understand who God is and who we are to become.

Ask: pray by asking God to reveal Himself to us and to expose any lie that we believed about Him, ourselves, and others. *Matthew21:22*, "If you believe, you will receive whatever you ask for in prayer." Therefore, ask for wisdom to understand.

Thanks: God has done so much for us and He is doing so much more in our lives, so we give Him thanks for the many blessings that are yet to come.

WRITE DOWN YOUR PRAYER PLAN HERE!

Start by praising God because of who He is, and the fact that you are here breathing, and still in your right state of mind.

PRAISING

Talk about some of the things that you are fighting yourself from doing, but never really find the courage to walk away from, and you need help

CONFESSION

Read the word of God or find someone to read it with you, to get a better understand of who God is, and what is expected of you.

READ THE WORD OF GOD

Ask God for wisdom to understand His word, and when you ask, believe and it shall be given to you.

ASK

And to close, even though you haven't seen the result yet, just give Him thanks because He will fulfills His promise

THANKS

IMPORTANT LIFE LESSON.

- ❖ Learn from others, but never become them.
- ❖ It's important to learn from people, but be yourself.
- ❖ The ultimate joy of life is knowing who you are.
- ❖ Lead with your life.
- ❖ Character will protect your words.
- ❖ Find your God-giving gift in life.
- ❖ Become a servant by letting your gift serve the world.
- ❖ Don't ever allow power, money, or sex control you.
- ❖ Temptation is only testing your character.
- ❖ Men or women of character don't have to say much.
- ❖ Remember you are here for a purpose.
- ❖ Love without commitment is just a feeling.
- ❖ Don't let what you do becomes who you are.
- ❖ Don't be discourage by the detours of life.
- ❖ Nobody is above counsel.
- ❖ Trust God enough to guide you.

STEP FOR SELF IMPROVEMENT

1. Change your negative self-talk to positive self-affirmation; you will only become what you believe about yourself, not what your teacher, your friend, or your family say about you, it's what you believe about yourself.
2. Don't be so hard on yourself, trust in your God-given ability, and work harder for yourself more than you work for others.
3. Be anxious of the things the world taught you but captivate what they fail to teach you.
4. Keep a positive attitude, because attitude is a product of belief.
5. Captivate your dreams and passions or you'll be enslaved because you can never retire from them.
6. What you were born to do is more powerful than what you have done.
7. Allow yourself to be a good soil where the dream inside of you finds room to grow.

ENCOURAGEMENT

Don't try to be like somebody else or comparing yourself with others. Be yourself otherwise you are a thief of yourself because you are stealing from who you are supposed to be in order to be like someone else. And if you're denying yourself by trying to be like someone else, then no one will be able to see you, how beautiful you are, and what you are capable of.

You have a gift; you have something to offer. Your gift, your passion, your dream, they are all waiting to be born, and it will take you and only you to give birth to them. So stop giving yourself reasons why you can't or shouldn't. Telling your story is not enough! Make it known to others, show it to the world, let them evaluate your God-given gift, we all have them, and I don't believe anyone is here by accident. You are here for a purpose and you were sent here with a plan in mind. Now you can choose to do something or nothing about it, but that doesn't mean it's not in you.

If you come across this book, may God use it to serve you well.

(We are here to serve)

126

COMMENTS,

IN THE BOOK OF HEBREWS 4:15, THE WRITER STATES: "FOR WE DO NOT HAVE A HIGH PRIEST WHO IS UNABLE TO EMPATHIZE WITH OUR WEAKNESSES, BUT WE HAVE ONE WHO HAS BEEN TEMPTED IN EVERY WAY, JUST AS WE ARE—YET HE DID NOT SIN." IN "LOVE WILL PREVAIL" BY DIEUNA AND LUTHER CHRISPIN, WE HAVE TWO PEOPLE WHO CAN SYMPATHIZE WITH OUR WEAKNESSES BECAUSE THEY HAVE ALSO EXPERIENCED WEAKNESSES, BUT THIS IS NOT A STORY ABOVE WEAKNESSES, BUT ABOVE VICTORY, VICTORY THAT IS ONLY FOUND IN AN ABIDING FAITH IN JESUS CHRIST OUR LORD. I RECOMMEND THIS STORY.

JOHN AND ISHA GRANT

LOVE WILL PREVAIL IS A BREATHTAKING LIFE STORY ABOUT LOVE, PASSION, FORGIVENESS, AND HOPE. MOST IMPORTANTLY, THE BOOK IS CENTERED AROUND THE LOVE OF CHRIST FOR HUMANITY AND HOW HE WILL ALWAYS BE VICTORIOUS

NATHALIE AND JHONNY CASSAMAJOR

LOVE WILL PREVAIL IS A STRAIGHT FOREWORD, HONEST, AND PERSONAL JOURNEY WITH GOD BY FAITH TO A HEALTHY MARRIAGE. IT'S AN EXCELLENT RELATIONSHIP BOOK FOR SINGLES AND COUPLES.

KILLICK AND MYRIAM DOLSAINT

FINDING TREASURE IN UNLIKELY PLACES

ONLY YOUR CONVICTION WILL MAKE YOUR DREAM COME TRUE, NOT SOMEONE ELSE'S CONVICTION ABOUT YOU.

We cannot change the fact that people will have their own opinion about who we are. But who we will be coming? Only God knows.

But the one thing we can do is having the right attitude towards ourselves and our future.

KEEP A POSITIVE THINKING TOWARDS YOUSELF, AND OTHERS. YOU CAN BE ALL THAT GOD CREATES YOU TO BE, WITH ALL THE POTENTIALS HE PLACED INSIDE OF YOU, NOT AROUND YOU. SO, DIG DEEP WITHIN TO FIND THE TREASURE HE PLACED IN YOU.

Printed in the United States
By Bookmasters